the secret life of
YOUR CAT

the secret life of
YOUR CAT

Unlock the mysteries of your pet's behaviour

VICKY HALLS

FIREFLY BOOKS

A FIREFLY BOOK

Published by Firefly Books Ltd. 2010

First printing

**Publisher Cataloging-in-Publication
Data (U.S.)**
Halls, Vicky.
The secret life of your cat : unlock the
mysteries of your pet's behavior / Vicky Halls.
[208] p. : col. photos. ; cm.
Includes index.
Summary: A look at the world through
feline eyes, with explanations of the cat's
character, its anatomy and its day-to-day
behavior.
ISBN-13: 978-1-55407-735-9 (pbk.)
ISBN-10: 1-55407-735-4 (pbk.)
1. Cats − Behavior. 2. Cats − Psychology. I.
Title.
636.8 dc22 SF446.5H355 2010

**Library and Archives Canada Cataloguing
in Publication**
A CIP record of this book is available from
Library and Archives Canada.

Published in the United States by
Firefly Books (U.S.) Inc.
P.O. Box 1338, Ellicott Station
Buffalo, New York 14205

Published in Canada by
Firefly Books Ltd.
66 Leek Crescent
Richmond Hill, Ontario L4B 1H1

Printed in China

Contents

Introduction

Cats have been part of our lives in one significant way or another for many thousands of years, and for most of that time we have struggled to truly understand them. Their behaviour can appear focused, manipulative and ruthless outdoors, yet loving and gentle with their owners at home. They can be contrary, fun-loving, dismissive and frolicsome in equal measure. So which cat is the real one?

Opposite Although we 'own' our domesticated cats, they resolutely remain the way nature made them, resisting attempts to fundamentally change them.

I doubt that we can ever domesticate the cat or even really claim to own a creature with such independence. It's a very telling fact that we have never succeeded in selectively breeding a cat to assist us humans by performing a particular role — there are no cats that can herd, guard or sniff on command. And we have failed to produce a cat that is significantly smaller or larger than nature's version, unlike the Chihuahua or the Great Dane in the case of our other favourite companion animal, the dog. The cat seems to defy any of our clumsy attempts to alter perfection or achieve a sense of control.

'A RIDDLE WRAPPED IN A MYSTERY INSIDE AN ENIGMA'

The more I study cats to discover the truth about their behaviour, the more I realize that we still only know half the story. Research is constantly revealing new and amazing facts about this incredible species, each piece of information linked with others to eventually complete the jigsaw puzzle. I continue in my quest to solve the mystery of the cat because the key to the wellbeing of the animal we love so much is in our understanding of it.

This book starts that journey of discovery by exploring the domestic cat's unique physiology to see how its structure contributes to its success as a species. We will then delve into the secretive world of its behaviour by getting close up and personal with the pet cat's 'wild' (feral) cousins to see how they spend their days. Domestic cats are only a whisker away from their wild side, so understand the wild cat and you'll get a little closer to understanding your own!

Throughout the book I refer to pet cats as male, for ease, so my apologies to anyone who shares their home with a female, as I do. It's nothing personal!

Knowing your cat inside out

The physical cat

We can only really appreciate another species if we understand their biology, so in order to get a feeling for what it is like to be a cat, here is an opportunity to find out what lies beneath the glossy fur.

All living organisms are categorized into class, order, family, genus and species. The domestic cat is classified as a carnivorous mammal of the Felidae family. This includes the sub-groups Felinae, Pantherinae and Acinonychinae. The Acinonychinae has a sole member, the cheetah, but the Pantherinae family includes the lion, tiger, panther and leopard. Felinae encompasses all the small cats, for example the lynx, serval, ocelot, caracal, jaguarundi, jungle cat and Pallas cat. Our own pet cat is a domesticated sub-species of *Felis silvestris* known as *F. silvestris catus*.

Certain aspects of the cat's anatomy and physiology have modified and adapted through the process of evolution to best suit its environment and role in nature. Whether a cat lives wild or in pampered luxury with a loving owner it's still built the same, and its ability and drive to behave in a particular way doesn't change. If you really want to get a true insight into your cat's behaviour (or at least what he should be doing instead of lying on his back in front of the fire), start with the basics by exploring how the domestic cat is constructed.

Getting to know your cat both inside and out will give you a small taste of what it must be like to be feline. Just a little information about what cats see, feel, hear and smell can be a revelation. They smell things we can't, like the odour of another cat that has passed through the garden. They hear ultrasonic sounds beyond the range of our own hearing. They feel vibration through their feet and whiskers so faint that we remain oblivious to it. Their heightened sensory abilities in comparison to our own lead many people to believe the myth that cats have a supernatural sixth sense. In reality, they are just so much more tuned into their surroundings than we are.

From the tip of the cat's nose to the end of its tail it possesses some unique features that together form one of the most successful and adaptable creatures of our time.

YOUR CAT'S PRIMARY SENSES

It's fitting that the first part of your cat we should explore is his nose, as he lives in a world dominated by odour, while a look at his eyes reveals his nocturnal lifestyle.

Your cat will use his nose in the same way you use your eyes and ears to read a newspaper or watch television to gain information about his

A cat's sense of smell is estimated to be 14 times stronger than that of a human. The nose pad, which is ridged with a unique finger-print-like pattern, is used to investigate textures and shapes as well.

environment, other animals, food and everything of importance in his territory. Cats have 200 million cells in their noses that are sensitive to odour, giving them a sense of smell estimated at 14 times stronger than that of a human. Your cat's nose is also sensitive to touch and temperature, and he uses it to investigate textures and shapes as well. The nose pad of each cat is ridged in a unique pattern, just like a human fingerprint.

Odours are so important to a cat's survival that they have a second organ of scent called the vomeronasal or Jacobson's organ, enabling them to 'taste' extremely significant smells. This organ consists of two small apertures behind the front teeth in the roof of the mouth that connect to the nasal cavity. The cat opens its mouth and draws the air into the apertures, which looks like a grimace and is referred to as the Flehmen response. Tom cats are frequently seen wearing this facial expression when they are searching for females in season by investigating any deposits of urine they may find, as the information gleaned will help them find a mate. Your cat's nose is particularly sensitive to odours containing nitrogen compounds, enabling him to sniff out and reject rancid or spoiled foods, which release chemicals rich in nitrogen.

Domestic as well as many wild cats respond to the smell of particular herbs and plants, driving them to rub their faces on them and to roll around and drool – similar to a male cat in response to a female in oestrous (on heat). The catnip plant (*Nepeta cataria*) contains the chemical trans-nepetalactone, closely related to a substance secreted by a queen (female cat) in her urine. Valerian can also produce the same effect.

Cats' eyes

Like most predators, your cat's eyes are located on the front of his head to aid the perception of depth when hunting. His field of vision is about 200 degrees, with a central section of binocular vision to help him judge distances. Feral cats tend to be long-sighted, compared to indoor cats, with vision tailored for prey that can be captured within running distance.

The cat is predominantly a nocturnal hunter, aided by a reflective membrane at the back of the eye called the *tapetum lucidum* that makes maximum use of low light conditions. Your cat's pupils are capable of dilating

All kittens are born with blue eyes. These change over time, becoming their final colour by the time they are 12 weeks of age.

DID YOU KNOW…?

- *All kittens are born with blue eyes, changing to their permanent colour by 12 weeks old.*

- *Cats have a third eyelid called the nictitating membrane that appears at the inner corner of the eye and closes to protect the eye from dryness and damage, saving the need to blink.*

- *Cats can't see objects clearly that are less than 20 cm (8 in) away.*

- *Most cats' eyes will glow silvery green when light is shone into them at night, but a Siamese's glow red!*

- *Your cat's eyes can function in about one-sixth of the light needed for human vision, but not in complete darkness.*

- *Cats' eyes are large in proportion to their head.*

to a diameter nearly twice as large as that of a human, which helps him further to see in semi-darkness. You will notice that his pupils constrict to a slit in bright light as a protective measure to avoid discomfort, common in mammals adapted to life in semi-darkness.

Pupil size not only changes according to the ambient light conditions but can also be a good indicator of a cat's mood: if your cat's feeling angry, he will have narrow pupils, while when he's excited or frightened by something, his eyes will be wide with fully dilated pupils.

Contrary to common belief, cats are not completely colour-blind. They can actually see blues, greens and yellows, although they can't distinguish red tones. But colour simply has no relevance to them in their lives as nocturnal hunters, when everything appears in shades of grey in any case.

Cats have a reflective membrane at the back of their eyes which enables them to make maximum use of low light conditions. In addition, their pupils can dilate nearly twice as much as humans' can.

THE CAT'S WHISKERS

Your cat uses his whiskers as an ingenious navigational tool, enabling him to know when he is near to an obstacle without needing to see it.

Your cat has 24 whiskers, called vibrissae, in rows on each side of his nose, with additional ones on each cheek, over the eyes, on the chin and on the back of each foreleg. They are twice as thick as ordinary cat hair, with roots embedded three times deeper into the surface of the skin. The roots of the whiskers extend deep into the follicles and have a large number of nerve endings at their base, making them extremely sensitive to wind speed, air pressure and touch. Any slight sensation on the tip of the cat's whisker will cause the eye to close as a reflex action to avoid injury from objects in the immediate vicinity while its attention is focused elsewhere.

A cat's whiskers are an important aid when it's hunting and manipulating its prey. As the cat is long-sighted it cannot see objects close up, so the whiskers move forward to accurately detect the position of prey. If a cat's whiskers have been cut or damaged, it will find it difficult to kill

The whiskers have many nerve endings at their bases which makes them very sensitive to air pressure, touch and wind speed. They can initiate a blink response to protect the eyes.

effectively. On the other hand, if a cat loses its sight, its whiskers will provide it with a form of 'vision' and enable it to adjust well to moving around in familiar surroundings.

Whiskers are also an indicator of a cat's mood. Your cat's whiskers will point slightly forwards and down when he's relaxed, lie flat on his face when he's being defensive and point forwards when he's being aggressive.

INSIDE YOUR CAT'S MOUTH

Teeth are the most important tool of the domestic cat as a predator, in order to catch and kill prey. They are also essential for defence against other cats.

Adult cats have 30 teeth, which are specialized for biting and tearing flesh. There are no grinding surfaces as cats don't chew their food but swallow it in chunks.

The adult cat has a total of 30 teeth: 12 incisors (the small teeth at the front of the jaw used mainly to help grooming), four canines (the long fang teeth used to catch and hold prey and deliver the fatal bite) and ten premolars and four molars (used for shearing meat to portions small enough to swallow). The first temporary set of 26 teeth appear in a kitten around two weeks of age, referred to as the milk or deciduous teeth. These are replaced by adult teeth around the age of six months.

Cats' teeth are highly specialized for biting and tearing flesh, fixed in a powerful jaw comprising the upper jaw, or maxilla, and the lower jaw, the mandible. Your cat has fewer molar teeth than most other mammals, with no grinding surfaces, as he doesn't chew his food but swallows it in chunks. He is able to feel the tiny depression at the back of the neck on his prey with his teeth so that he knows where to bite.

Cats have bacteria in their mouths called *Pasteurella multocida* that are the cause of most cat bite abscesses when they fight. This bacterium won't cause a problem in your cat's mouth, but if injected into the bloodstream of another cat when a canine tooth punctures the skin it will potentially result in infection. All cat bite wounds to people should be treated straight away for the same reason, so a visit to your doctor is recommended.

In the wild, a cat's teeth are cleaned as they scrape them over the bones of their prey. Your pet cat, fed on a commercial cat food, does not have this opportunity and can experience a build-up of plaque and tartar on his teeth, leading to gum and dental disease. If your cat has difficulty in eating, bad breath and excessive salivation, it could indicate discomfort associated with dental disease.

Tongue and taste

Anyone who has ever been licked by a cat will know that its tongue is surprisingly rough! Its abrasive surface is covered with over a thousand tiny tooth-like spines called papillae made from keratin, the same material that makes human fingernails. These are shaped like hooks, enabling the cat to remove fur and feathers and clean off any flesh from the bones of its prey. The spines on your cat's tongue also make it an incredibly efficient tool to smooth and untangle his fur when he grooms. Your cat will also use his tongue to cover his fur with saliva in order to cool him down as it evaporates. There's no need to towel dry your cat either, as he will use his tongue to lick away any wetness.

Your cat also uses his tongue for drinking in a novel way by curling it like a spoon and scooping the liquid up and backwards into his mouth, only swallowing every third or fourth lap.

The cat's sense of taste has evolved to focus on their specialist carnivorous diet. Although compared to humans it is weak, a cat still responds predominantly to sour, bitter and salt, with little if any response to sweet. Your cat makes up for this deficiency with a superior sense of smell when it comes to food. That's why cats with flu symptoms and a blocked nose go off their food and need strong-smelling treats to stimulate their appetite.

The area of the brain that controls balance, posture and movement is the cerebellum. It is large in cats so it is unsurprising that cats are so fleet-of-foot and graceful.

INSIDE YOUR CAT'S BRAIN

Studying the cat's brain and the proportionate sizes of its different areas gives us humans a valuable insight into what the species is all about.

The physical structure of your cat's brain is very similar to your own, consisting of three main sections: the forebrain, the midbrain and the hindbrain. The cerebellum in the hindbrain is large in the cat and therefore of some significance. As this area controls the coordination of balance, posture and movement, it's no surprise that your cat is born to climb, twist, move gracefully and land on his feet when he falls.

The cerebral cortex in the forebrain, known as the 'seat' of intelligence, contains areas that receive information from sensory receptors in the body and control movement. The specialized nature of the cat is apparent here too, as the area associated with hearing is large; acute hearing is essential when hunting small prey.

The cerebral cortex is described as the 'new' part of the brain where behaviour is learned and developed in a sophisticated way. There are, however, older parts of the brain in all three sections that have a construction common to all mammals. These areas control the instinctive and innate behaviour like eating and drinking and the intense emotions that are 'hard-wired' such as aggression, rage and fear.

While some of your cat's behaviour is instinctive, he will also learn a wide range of responses during his lifetime. Cats learn by observing or imitating others and by trial and error. Humans are constantly trying to establish quite how intelligent cats are, but this is impossible if they are assessed according to a human perspective. It's wiser to judge an animal's intelligence by its ability to use and understand its environment, and adapt to new ones. By this measure, cats are very intelligent indeed!

HOW YOUR CAT FEELS

Scientists now accept that animals have emotions, and that includes your cat. Previously thought to feel only the primitive emotions of fear and aggression, advances in neuroscience show that they can experience more complex feelings.

Cats are capable of feeling positive and negative emotions, each on a scale that can vary from pleasure to ecstasy and apprehension to terror.

Play is highly enjoyable to cats. Such pleasurable activity releases the hormone dopamine in the brain, which gives them a sense of wellbeing.

The limbic system is the part of the brain buried under the cerebral cortex that controls emotions and motivations, particularly those essential for your cat's survival, such as fear, anger and the pleasurable feelings associated with food and sexual behaviour. The hypothalamus, part of this limbic system, is responsible for controlling emotions, food and water intake, the sleep-wake cycle and many other functions that maintain his body's equilibrium. One of its functions is to control hormones through the endocrine system.

In fact, it's impossible to talk about the brain, intelligence and emotions without bringing the hormones into the frame, as they play an important role when your cat reacts emotionally. The adrenal gland found near the kidneys is particularly significant in his body's response to stress. It produces adrenalin, which fuels the 'fight or flight' response to danger, and a steroid hormone called cortisol that adjusts your cat's metabolism at times of mental and physical stress. Chronic unavoidable stress can lead to constantly high levels of cortisol in his bloodstream, causing changes to the immune response and an increased susceptibility to disease.

One of the emotions that you want your cat to experience is pleasure. You will recognize this state of mind when your cat curls up next to you, purring and treading with his front paws. Play is also a highly enjoyable experience; the physical exertion of play releases a hormone in the brain called dopamine that gives your cat a sense of wellbeing. This is a little like the experience you might have after a workout at the gym! However, it's not always that easy to determine a cat's emotional state. As they are not fundamentally social creatures, they have no intrinsic need to signal emotion with their body language and facial expression, particularly if that emotion could put them at a disadvantage and make them vulnerable to attack.

HEARING AND BALANCE

Your cat's sense of balance, movement and hearing are finely tuned to catch small prey, the latter acute enough to judge within 7.5 cm (3 in) the location of a sound 90 cm (3 ft) away.

The hearing range of the cat extends from 48 hertz to 85 kilohertz, compared to ours of a mere 20 hertz to 20 kilohertz, making it the broadest of any mammal. The cat's rodent prey emits a high-pitched squeak, hence the need to increase the range of its hearing, but this has occurred during the course of its evolution without sacrificing the ability to hear low-frequency sounds. Your cat will therefore also be responsive to the high pitch

of the female voice, and can hear sounds up to 1.6 octaves higher than our ears can. Even dogs can't compete at this range!

In your cat's inner ear, deep within the skull, is a group of semicircular canals that form the vestibular system. These canals are filled with fluid and sensory hairs that enable him to balance and move with great precision. This aids one of your cat's most famous attributes, the ability to right himself when falling to safely land on all four feet.

Your cat's outer ears, called the pinnae, are comparatively large and controlled by 32 separate muscles, compared to our paltry six, allowing them to rotate independently through 180 degrees to turn towards the direction of the slightest sound.

The angle of your cat's ears is an important indicator of mood, showing fear when they are flattened against his head, anger when they are rotated backwards and excitement when they are pricked upright and slightly forwards.

The Scottish and American Fold breeds of cat possess a genetic mutation that makes their ear cartilage contain a fold, causing the ears to bend forwards and down towards the front of the head. Cats with white fur and pale skin on their ears are particularly prone to sunburn, so take precautionary measures if this is the case with your cat, as frequent sunburn can lead to skin cancer. Or has he even got two sets of ears? This can be the result of a rare genetic mutation, first studied in 1957.

The cats' hearing range is the broadest of any mammal, encompassing both low- and high-frequency sounds. Their large outer ears can rotate independently through 180 degrees.

THE BARE BONES

As a self-reliant creature, your cat needs to be able to maintain his own coat in good order and groom from top to tail, which would be impossible without his incredible degree of flexibility.

Hunting, climbing, jumping and generally behaving like a cat requires a considerable amount of dexterity and agility. The way your cat's whole body is constructed contributes to that supreme flexibility, but the skeleton provides the all-important foundation. Your cat has approximately 250 bones, depending on the length of his tail, held together by muscles, ligaments and tendons to form the skeleton. Extra thoracic and lumbar vertebrae in his spine, in combination with greater movement between each individual vertebra, give your cat his unique bending and flexing potential. Your cat's skeleton is supported by long, lean muscles that give him his jumping prowess and ability to run in brief bursts at speeds up to 30 mph (48 kph). He is not, however, built for endurance; he's only very fast and strong over short distances. The cat is definitely a sprinter, not a marathon runner!

Your cat doesn't possess a collarbone, but instead has 'free-floating' clavicles that enable the forelimbs to rotate to almost any angle, giving him maximum mobility. Anyone who has ever left a window open just a tiny amount will know that it's enough to allow a cat through; if your cat can squeeze his head through a gap, then you know his body can follow!

The cat's skull is shortened in comparison with most carnivores, but the correspondingly shorter lower jaw (mandible) enhances the action of the muscles that close it to increase the force of the killer bite. Certain pedigrees, such as the Siamese and its derivatives, have an elongated skull, referred to as doliocephalic. Persians and similar breeds have a very different appearance, with a shortened skull and a nose that has been pushed back and up in line with the eyes in some extreme varieties. This is referred to as a brachycephalic skull.

Opposite When compared with those of other carnivores, cats' skulls are shortened, although relatively speaking some pedigrees such as Siamese have an elongated – or doliocephalic – skull.

INTERNAL NETWORKING

In common with all mammals, your cat has a number of complex internal body systems that work together. These systems have various adaptations that help to reinforce his specialized lifestyle.

Your cat's structural systems include the skeleton, muscles, skin and cardiovascular, or circulatory, system (transports blood around the body). The visceral systems include the digestive system (converts food to energy), respiratory system (takes in oxygen and expels carbon dioxide), urinary system (removes waste and surplus water) and the reproductive system (to ensure the future of the species). Your cat's body also requires two coordinating systems, nervous and endocrine, to receive and relay information and enable all the systems to communicate properly with each other. Your cat also possesses other highly specialized systems, such as the immune system and the lymphatic system, both of which play a role in his body's battle against disease.

A cat's digestive system is adapted to process frequent small meals throughout a 24-hour period. Being what is known as an obligate carnivore, your cat converts protein from a meat source for energy, which means that he can't survive on a vegetarian diet.

Your cat's urinary tract is specialized to accommodate a minimal water intake. This is because the domestic cat is descended from the desert-dwelling African Wildcat (*Felis silvestris lybica*) and has maintained its ancestor's adaptation to a dry environment. Consequently, your cat has a decreased response to thirst and can survive on less water than a dog, ignoring mild levels of dehydration with ease. Cats compensate for this by producing very concentrated urine in comparison to that of humans.

EXTERNAL ASSETS

A cat's coat is true fur, with primary (guard) hairs and secondary hairs of awn and down, also known as wool. Your cat may have a thin skin, but its looseness is highly protective.

The guard hairs of your cat's fur grow singly from individual follicles surrounded by other follicles, with several secondary hairs growing from each one. These guard hairs are surrounded by tiny muscles that tense to make your cat's hair stand on end at will. This gives your cat increased insulation when it's cold and also makes him look larger and therefore scarier to a potential adversary. The thickness of the fur will vary according to the seasonal temperature, which means that your cat's coat will moult regularly, when new hair pushes out the old.

Opposite Selective breeding in cats such as in this white Cornish Rex often concentrates on variations in the proportions of the three hair types that make up cat fur: guard hairs, awn and down.

Selective breeding has often concentrated on variations in the cat's coat, with some pedigrees utilizing all three hair types in different proportions and others only having one or two types. The Angora, for example, has less-developed down hair, while the Persian has down hair as long as its guard hairs. Some pedigrees have mutant coats that deviate a very long way from the norm, such as the Cornish Rex, which lacks guard hairs and its awn and down hairs are curly. The La Perm has a longer coat of curls and waves resembling an old-fashioned, shaggy perm. The Sphynx has probably the most extreme example of a mutant coat – merely a thin covering of down.

Your cat's skin is covered in sensory receptors that feed messages to the brain relating to touch, heat, cold, pressure and pain. His skin is loose in comparison to most animals, allowing him to turn and twist to confront his attacker, even if the latter has a firm grip. It also means that the potentially deep penetrative wounds inflicted by the canine teeth of another cat can remain fairly superficial. The loose skin at the back of the neck, called the scruff, is used by the mother cat to carry her kittens from one nest to another. The kitten's natural response is to go limp when carried in this way to enable safe transportation. Although this is a natural reflex in the young, humans should not attempt to mimic this, either for restraint or carrying, as it can be very uncomfortable.

A cat's hind paws each have four toes, while the forepaws consist of five. The fifth toe is held slightly off the ground and is referred to as the dewclaw.

YOUR CAT'S EXTREMITIES

Your cat walks on his toes (referred to as digitigrade) in a precise manner, with each hind paw placed in the print of the corresponding forepaw, and uses his tail in his balancing act.

Cats are also capable of walking with both left legs, then both right legs, rather than following a pattern of alternates. If your cat wants to move faster, he uses diagonally opposite legs simultaneously. Your cat has five toes on each forepaw and four on each hind paw. The fifth toe on his forepaw is slightly off the ground and referred to as the dewclaw. He also has sweat glands that produce watery sweat on the foot pads. This is secreted when your cat is hot or frightened, but doesn't have much of a cooling effect. A small pad on your cat's wrist called the carpal or stopper pad is thought to be an anti-skidding device used while jumping. The thick pads on the foot act as shock absorbers when landing and insulation against extremes of temperature.

Cats do not follow a pattern of alternates when they walk, but lift both left, then both right legs. If they want to move fast they can use diagonally opposite legs simultaneously.

Opposite The domestic cat is the only feline species that can hold its tail vertically while walking. The tail is used as an aid to balancing and is also an important indicator of mood.

Like all feline species, apart from the cheetah, cats have protractable claws that remain withdrawn in a protective sheath of skin and fur when they are relaxed. This prevents wear and keeps them sharp and ready for hunting, climbing or self-defence when needed. The claws on the forepaws are sharper than those on the hind paws, and are maintained by scratching (stropping) on vertical or horizontal surfaces to remove the outer husks. Your cat keeps his hind claws in good order by chewing them. Claws are made from keratin, the same protein that forms the outer layer of the skin.

When your cat is a happy cat, he will 'knead' with his claws on blankets or clothing. This harks back to his early experience as a kitten, when he kneaded at its mother's teat to stimulate milk production.

The tail end

The bones of the tail, called the caudal vertebrae, make up ten per cent of the total number of bones in your cat's skeleton. Your cat uses his tail as an aid to balancing; for example, if he is walking on a narrow surface and moves his head, his tail will automatically move in the opposite direction to maintain stability. Your cat uses the caudal vertebrae in his tail as a counterbalance to his body during quick movements to maintain speed while changing direction in pursuit of prey. When it's cold, your cat will wear his tail like a scarf, wrapping it round his body to cover his nose.

As a result of a complicated and efficient combination of ligaments, tendons and muscles, the domestic cat is the only feline species to be able to hold its tail vertically while walking. All the species of wild cat hold their tail horizontally or tucked under. The Manx cat is tailless or has a stumpy tail as a result of a genetic mutation that affects the entire spine, causing malformation or fusing or, in extreme cases, spina bifida.

Your cat communicates with others through body posture and his tail plays an important role in conveying his mood. If your cat is content, he will greet a familiar human with a raised tail; if he's particularly excited he will quiver the tip of his tail. Your cat will also use the raised tail mode to signal to a friendly cat prior to mutual rubbing. If your cat wags his tail, thrashing it from side to side, it spells conflict and frustration, and may end in an act of aggression. A constantly twitching tail tip shows that your cat is mildly irritated; cats in pain will often flick their tails in this way. If your cat is fearful, his tail will be low and his fur will be puffed up. An aggressive cat will have its tail held horizontally with an arched base.

DID YOU KNOW…?

- *Cats can voluntarily extend their claws on one or more paws.*

- *Domestic and feral cats are prone to a form of paw mutation called polydactylism and may have six or seven toes.*

- *The protractor muscles in older cats weaken and their claws are often permanently visible, so trimming regularly will prevent them catching in carpets, fabrics or skin.*

- *Declawing (onychectomy) removes the last joint of the cat's toes as well as the claw, and although still legal in North America, it's a prohibited practice in the UK and most other countries.*

- *If you gently press the top and bottom of your cat's paws, the claws will extend to ease trimming.*

A walk on the wild side

Feral cats

Have you ever wondered how your cat would cope without you? Feral cats live independently of humans yet are, in every other respect, the same species as those that live happily in our homes.

The process of domestication of the cat has taken many thousands of years, but achieved comparatively little modification of the species. We have, despite our best efforts, failed to produce a cat that deviates, either in size or shape, too greatly from its wild ancestor. Even the most pampered pet can, given the right set of circumstances, vote with its paws and 'go native' by reverting to a life without humans. Most cats are capable of accessing that fundamental 'hard-wiring' to live like their feral cousins.

A feral cat is very different by definition from a stray or pet cat. Although of domestic cat origin, a truly feral cat is one born and reared in the wild with no contact with humans. Feral cats populate most of the world in a vast array of different environments and climates, giving further weight to the argument that the domestic feline is one of the world's most adaptable creatures. However, the life of a feral cat is tough and comparatively short, with a life expectancy of, on average, five years against 12–15 for a pet cat.

Truly feral cats are born and reared in the wild with no contact at all with humans. Life is tough for feral cats: their life expectancy is about five years, as compared with the 12–15 years for domestic cats.

Feral cats are in essence the same as domestic cats, living their lives in the same way as your cat would were you not there. Understanding feral cats can give you an insight into your cat's behaviour.

In some continents the domestic cat is a top-of-the-food-chain predator; in others it's preyed upon by animals such as wolves, bears and snakes. Although it is impossible to be sure of the true numbers, there are an estimated one million feral cats in the UK and the Humane Society of the United States suggests a figure of 50 million feral cats in the USA.

In every aspect the feral cat is exactly the same species living in the same way *your* cat would if you weren't around. If feral kittens are hand-reared from an early age, for example, they can adapt reasonably well and adjust to life as a pet. Therefore, understanding the feral cat, its social communication, routines and motivations, will potentially give you an insight into your own cat's behaviour and a glimpse of what he might be up to when he goes through the cat flap every morning. Even if the closest your cat gets to the great outdoors is gazing through a window, you can at least start to appreciate what he may be thinking!

Opposite Small
mammals are feral
cats' main source of
food since they hunt
to survive. Although
they prefer to hunt
at dawn and dusk,
they will adapt
according to the
availability of prey.

THE HUNTER-SCAVENGER

Feral cats, living without interference or assistance from man, hunt prey to survive. They are rodent specialists, preferring to hunt at dawn and dusk when their chosen targets are at their most active.

Cats can, however, adapt to hunting at other times to suit the prey type available or if the opportunity arises. They adapt easily to living and hunting in open countryside and woodland, and cope least well in areas where their prey disappears in the winter. Having evolved in a warm, dry climate, cats that inhabit a cold, damp environment can survive, but tend to have shorter, harder lives. Despite the reputation of the cat as a prolific killer, there are many ferals that are malnourished, unable to catch enough food, even eating carrion and road kill rather than go hungry.

Cats are often considered to be responsible for a depletion of the bird population, but small mammals remain their primary food source, although in low-latitude countries reptiles form a significant part of their diet. In studies carried out throughout the world, predation on birds was calculated and found to represent only 4–18 per cent of the cat's total food intake.

Rabbits, rodents and rubbish

Depending on the availability of prey, cats will hunt for up to 12 hours and can travel over a mile (1.6 km), there and back, for a single hunting excursion. Life is hard for the feral, taking as long as 70 minutes to catch one mouse at times when prey is scarce. Young rabbits are seasonally popular (adult rabbits in hard winters), as they weigh on average ten times more than a typical rodent but take only five times longer to catch. The feral will always choose the option that produces the maximum return for the minimum effort.

With the harsh reality of hunting for survival, an opportunistic approach to feeding is an essential strategy for the feral cat and historically a significant contributor to their willingness to live in close proximity to man. Feral cats congregate in colonies in populated areas to take advantage of the predictable and plentiful supply of human food waste. Rodents thrive in these areas too, resulting in a first-class source of sustenance for the feral 'family' from abundant prey as well as rich pickings from scavenging.

Cats possess specialist hunting skills that rely on visual and auditory cues. They can detect the telltale scratching noises and high-pitched squeaks of their prey and accurately pinpoint the source of the sound. They then lock onto the prey visually in response to its movement, although experienced cats can easily recognize immobile prey.

Go prowling or wait in ambush?

Cats hunt using two basic strategies depending on the chosen prey species, the time of day, weather and their own health and level of fitness. The first strategy, referred to as 'mobile' or 'stalk, run, pounce', requires the cat to move around an area, seeking out prey visually.

Once a target is identified, the cat will freeze, then slowly lower its body and head to the ground and stalk its intended victim, often using the cover of grass and vegetation. It moves extremely slowly and silently, pausing occasionally to avoid detection. Its ears are pointed forwards and its eyes fixed on its prey. Once the cat reaches the appropriate distance it pounces, pushing off with its hind legs and landing its front paws on the prey. Hunting for birds requires the stalking strategy, as they have an excellent field of vision and are aware of danger from every angle.

The other strategy, known as 'stationary, sit, wait' or 'ambush', is more appropriate for rodents and rabbits and requires the cat to crouch, sit or stand motionless adjacent to a burrow (or place where prey has previously been sighted) and pounce when it appears. Cats can remain for a couple of hours outside burrows waiting for the unfortunate occupants to emerge.

Once caught, to prevent the prey from escaping or attempting to fight back, the cat will often 'play' with it and toss it from paw to paw to ensure that it's stunned. The cat then delivers a bite to the back of the neck that severs the spinal cord and kills it instantly. Larger victims are suffocated by a powerful clamping bite on the throat. The cat then either consumes its kill immediately, caches it in a safe spot to eat later or carries it back to its den, particularly if it's a female with young to feed.

TERRITORY IS ALL...

The cat is instinctively territorial yet its requirements for territory differ depending on whether it's a solitary individual hunting for prey to survive or a colony member in an area with abundant food.

A cat's territory consists of the area that contains everything it needs to survive and thrive. Within the territory will be places to hunt, sleep and eat without interference. The cat's core area or 'den' is sheltered and safe from danger, and is the place where it can sleep undisturbed, eat and rest between hunting forays. This chosen patch will change from time to time in the interests of enhanced security and to prevent any build-up of parasites. The core area for the female with kittens is the nest where the kittens are born and reared. This too will change as mothers move their offspring from one site to another.

While this core area forms the hub of the territory, there is an area beyond it that the solitary cat will actively defend against invasion by others, called the home range. The size of this area will vary depending on the gender of the individual, the season, the availability of prey or scavenged food and the density of the surrounding cat population.

Beyond the boundaries of the defended home range is the entire area over which the cat will roam and hunt for food, referred to as the hunting range. This is also of variable size depending on the same factors that influence the home range. Within the whole territory the cat will have established paths and thoroughfares that are well trodden, often at specific times, especially if the density of the cat population is high. Throughout the territory the cat will leave its own scent marks and investigate those of others (see pages 40–41 for more about scent communication). Scent is used in this way to signal sexual availability or to establish access rights in an area of particular importance.

Once a territory is established, the only time a cat will ever venture outside it is for mating or if the resources within it become permanently depleted. During breeding season male cats may range further than usual.

...BUT SIZE ISN'T EVERYTHING

The size of a feral cat's territory depends on the availability of food and whether or not that food can be acquired only by cooperating with other cats as part of a group or colony.

Urban-dwelling feral cats often live in colonies and congregate in areas where people have created an abundance of eating opportunities.

Urban-dwelling feral cats often live in such family groups, as scavenging and direct feeding from well-meaning humans provides them with a dependable and plentiful supply of food. In these situations, according to a study of urban feral cats, a female's territory may be as small as 0.2 hectares (½ acre), with little need to venture further to find food to nourish herself and any offspring. The male's territory, reported in the same study, would extend to around 2 hectares (5 acres). The male's territory is always greater, as they live on the periphery of the predominantly matriarchal colony and range further afield for breeding. Male home ranges will often overlap those of females so that mating potential is on hand, but they will leave their own home range and travel some distance in the pursuit of a female on heat.

These 'urbanized' feral cats that make good use of our human food bounty can tolerate living at a relatively high population density, which in reality means 30 or more cats per 0.4 hectares (1 acre). This compares to pet cats in a similar urban setting that often live at a density of over 50 cats per 0.4 hectares (1 acre), being totally controlled by their owners and the proximity of other housing, much of which will be inhabited by multiple cats.

Subgroups of two or more cats sometimes exist within a larger colony, with group members spending time together and exhibiting signs of genuine friendship.

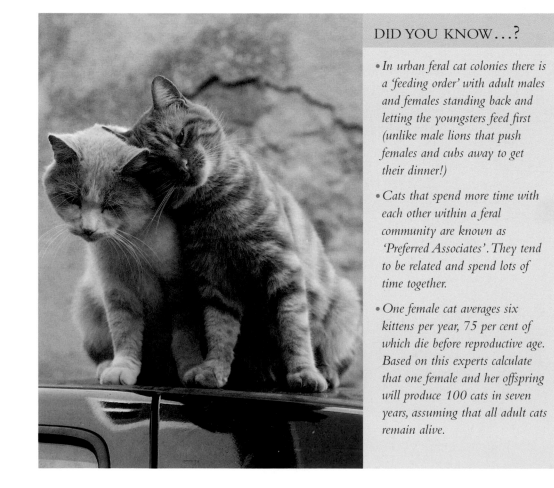

DID YOU KNOW...?

• *In urban feral cat colonies there is a 'feeding order' with adult males and females standing back and letting the youngsters feed first (unlike male lions that push females and cubs away to get their dinner!)*

• *Cats that spend more time with each other within a feral community are known as 'Preferred Associates'. They tend to be related and spend lots of time together.*

• *One female cat averages six kittens per year, 75 per cent of which die before reproductive age. Based on this experts calculate that one female and her offspring will produce 100 cats in seven years, assuming that all adult cats remain alive.*

Rural feral cats don't have the same opportunity to scavenge or rely on cat lovers to supply food. Being dependent on hunting for survival, they require a territory that's large enough to provide prey species in sufficient numbers to fulfil their nutritional needs. In a study of feral cats in Australia, it was found that the adults maintained specific home ranges of on average 6.2 km² (2½ miles²) for the male and 1.7 km² (¾ mile²) for the female. The density of the cat population was 2.4 per km² (1 mile²) in the summer, falling to 0.74 per km² (¼ mile²) in the winter, perhaps as a result of lack of food for the youngsters or becoming the prey of other species.

Fighting is rare within a feral colony unless resources are very scarce. Instead, group members often engage in social behaviours such as grooming each other.

THE FERAL FAMILY

Although cats don't actually need to develop social relationships to survive, there are circumstances when living in a group enables the individual to tap into a particular, valuable food source.

Feral colonies, made up predominantly of related females and their offspring, congregate in areas where humans have created an abundance of eating opportunities. This can take the form of scavenging, for example from refuse containers outside hotels or hospitals, with no intent on the part of humans to provide them with sustenance, or a kindly cat lover committed to feeding at regular intervals with the sole purpose of nourishing and maintaining the colony. The amount of food available and the quantity and quality of other significant resources in the area will greatly influence the size of the group that forms.

Within the group the cats will engage in social behaviour including rubbing and grooming each other. This behaviour is referred to as

A cat uses the scent glands in its face to mark its territory. This scent marking will also provide the cat with a sense of familiarity and security within its range.

allorubbing and allogrooming and it enables the scent of the two cats to be mixed and the communal odour of the colony to be maintained. It's this recognized group scent that binds them all together. Within each colony subgroups of two or more cats may exist that spend a lot of time together and show genuine signs of friendship. The females cooperatively rear the kittens in the colony, and as the males reach adolescence, they normally leave or remain on the outskirts of the group. Fighting is rare within a colony, unless the resources are scarce. If the availability of food declines, the group will eventually disperse to search elsewhere for better pickings.

More dominant personalities will make their presence felt within each group, but cats, unlike dogs, don't have a structured and defined hierarchy when they live together. There is no agreed 'pecking order' and no specific body language or behaviour associated with the acknowledgment of a hierarchy. The oldest female may have the equivalent of an 'alpha' status, with privileged access to resources, but any competitive dispute between other individuals over resources will be a straight win or lose contest resolved on the day.

IT'S THE WAY THEY SAY IT

Cats evolved to be solitary predators, so they don't want or need company when they hunt. Most of a cat's communication in its territory is about increasing distance between individuals, not encouraging approaches.

As cats patrol their territory they deposit their unique odour by rubbing scent glands in their faces, flanks, tail base and paws on various surfaces such as trees, bushes and pathways. Very little is known about the true purpose of this marking, but it clearly provides information that can be 'read' by other cats. Scent marking also gives the depositor a sense of familiarity and relative security in certain areas of its range.

When cats rub their faces on objects, it indicates that they feel familiar with a particular environment or social situation. They will use their chin, cheek or forehead, depending on the object they intend to anoint. The glands in the paws deposit scent when a cat scratches, so in this way it leaves both a visual indicator and an odour in areas of great significance in its territory. These marks are often found on the edges of a cat's territory, as well as at especially important sites within it.

Can you spray that again?

Scent marking with urine is referred to as spraying. The cat, when observed, may sniff a vertical surface first before turning and backing up towards it in a standing posture with its tail upright. A small jet of urine is then deposited while the cat quivers its tail and treads with its back paws to stretch and raise its back end as high as possible. In sexually active males and females, the urine marks communicate their availability for mating, with males spraying more frequently than females.

Cats will normally bury their faeces, but under certain circumstances they may deposit them in a strategically important open area as a form of marking, known as middening. This usually occurs at the boundaries of a cat's territory or in the centre of a pathway that may be the subject of dispute between cats competing for territory.

Sexually active cats communicate their availability to mate by scent marking, which they do by spraying urine. Male cats spray more than females do.

Coming head to head

Unfortunately, it isn't always possible for the free-roaming cat to avoid contact with others and there may be occasions when two cats meet face to face. The cat's ultimate survival depends on it remaining healthy enough to hunt and defend itself, so actively fighting is avoided unless absolutely necessary. Direct communication has to rely on something more dramatic and immediate than scent.

Cats use both visual displays and vocalization to convey their intentions. Each cat uses a complex sequence of body language and postures at this stage to ensure that the other cat thinks twice before embarking on a fight. It's a tense game of bluff and counter-bluff as both cats attempt to avoid conflict and leave the scene without losing face. Cats have no obvious signals of submission or appeasement, as they haven't evolved to rely on hierarchy and a pack structure to survive. Therefore, in the face of an aggressor, a cat will adopt a defensively aggressive posture in an attempt to dissuade the former from actually attacking.

Defensive and offensive aggression is signalled in the ears, eyes, tail and body position. For example, an aggressor will approach its victim sideways on, with lowered head, narrowed unblinking eyes and raised hindquarters. The tail may have a slight arch at the base, but be held horizontally or slightly towards the ground. The cat may also be vocalizing with a low snarl or growl. The defender will crouch down or lie on its back ready to use all four legs to counter the attack and rake at the belly of the aggressor. Its eyes will be wide with dilated pupils and its ears will be flat against its head with its mouth open, hissing. If the defender has the ability to escape, and the aggressor feels it has made its point, then a slow withdrawal with head lowered and no eye contact will take place. The aggressor will, for a while, look disinterested until the defender suddenly feels that enough ground is between them and runs for its life. The aggressor makes a half-hearted attempt to chase as a confirming gesture that it's definitely won the dispute.

FIGHTING TOOTH AND CLAW

Most direct contact between unfamiliar cats results in body language used specifically to avoid physical conflict. But when aggressor meets aggressor and neither will back down, it's inevitable that a serious fight will ensue.

Males are more likely to fight than females and disputes are often related to competition over access to females for mating or territory. Two tomcats that are equally matched will stand very close to each other, almost touching, and maintain direct eye contact. They

---

DID YOU KNOW...?

- Abscesses caused by cat bites are one of the most common injuries treated at veterinary practices.

- Aggression towards other cats is either partially or totally suppressed if a male cat is castrated during the first year of life.

- Research has shown that the orange allele (one of a pair of genes controlling coat colour) may be linked to aggressiveness in males, so beware the ginger tom!

remain in this position for several minutes, tense and frozen still, with one or both of them emitting an intense wailing sound. Suddenly, in a split second, one will adjust his ear carriage to rotate backwards, a strong indicator that physical attack is imminent. The aggressor will then attempt to bite the neck of his opponent. In that same split second, his adversary will have detected the signal of attack and rolled onto his back to release the weaponry of the four limbs with the view to restraining his adversary with the forelegs and raking his underbelly with the hind claws.

The speed at which the fighting takes place is incredible as the cats roll on the ground, each trying to assume the raking posture or complete the neck bite depending on the opportunity. If one cat remains in the defensive posture for long enough, it may be sufficient to prevent the aggressor from further attacks and the two will break. A mutual understanding will have occurred that one is the victor and they will move away. Serious and potentially fatal injury can arise from bite wounds that become infected and cause septicaemia (blood poisoning). Bite wounds are also the main transmission route for feline immunodeficiency virus (FIV), a retrovirus that is endemic in the domestic cat population throughout the world.

Some fighting can take place that appears inhibited in comparison. This usually involves powerful, rapid slaps to the face and body with alternate forepaws as well as bites, but serious damage is usually avoided by the opponents twisting to avoid bites, then separating and escaping at the first opportunity. Superficial cuts and scratches are common, and most tomcats carry the scars of fighting on their faces and ears.

Males are more likely to fight than females, and research indicates that ginger toms may be more aggressive than cats with other coat colours.

THE BIRDS AND THE BEES

In most areas domestic cats commonly have two litters a year. Females have several oestrus cycles during particular seasons, the main one being early spring in the Northern hemisphere.

During this period, females typically cycle at 15-day intervals unless they conceive. In areas where feral cats are solitary, the males will roam some distance outside their home range to seek opportunities to mate. In communal-living cats, the males are reluctant to limit their mating activity to just one group of females if others can be found in relative proximity.

The male's mating success is related to his age and weight, giving him 'dominance' over other males competing for access to females on heat. However, that same 'winning' male may be defeated by a lighter, younger male if he should encroach on females from a separate group where the other male is resident. Males don't, however, maintain exclusive mating territories. Weaker, subordinate males tend to stay close to home and mate with receptive females when other males aren't around. This creates a tendency towards inbreeding, as colonies are predominantly familial groups. But females from groups where there are resident males leave home more often during oestrous than those without males in attendance.

The wanton female

Female cats will mate willingly with most males. A female courted by a number of males is sometimes able to break up disputes between males to avoid one dominant male from monopolizing the opportunities to copulate. The latter can occur 15–20 times per 24 hours during the four to five days of oestrous, and the female will increase scent marking during this time to attract as many males as possible. Although the most assertive male will still have the most successful matings, others will also succeed and fights between the males-in-waiting at this time are minimal.

With this apparent promiscuity, it's no surprise to learn that the domestic cat is not a monogamous species and that no pair bonding takes place between breeding individuals. The female mates with multiple tomcats and will potentially give birth to kittens from each of them in the same litter.

From copulation to kitten

Shortly before coming into season the female will scent mark by rubbing against prominent objects in the territory and spraying urine, indicating that she's ready to mate. She makes a distinctive wailing sound, rolls on her back and crouches with her tail angled to one side in preparation for mating in a posture known as 'lordosis'.

The male cat then mounts her, grooming the back of her head, before grasping the scruff of her neck in his jaws. Copulation is brief and as the tomcat pulls away the queen cries in pain as backward-pointing barbs on the male's penis scrape against the vagina, triggering the release of the hormones

Opposite Cats are not monogamous and no pair bonding occurs. Females can mate with multiple tomcats, potentially giving birth to kittens from each in the same litter.

that stimulate ovulation. After a period of 24 hours following mating the sperm from the male reaches the eggs and fertilization takes place.

Towards the end of the 63-day gestation period, the female searches for a safe haven to deliver her kittens. Feral cats make their nests in places that are dry, private and perceived as out of harm's way including thickets, tree hollows or rock piles. As labour starts the mother cat becomes restless, moving constantly and licking her vulva. Kittens may take anything from one to 50 minutes to be born and the litter size can be between one and ten kittens, with an average of four or five. Kittens are born in their placenta, which the mother removes and then eats. She clears any mucus from each kitten's nose and mouth to clear its airway and licks it dry.

In colonies, females often act as midwives during the birth of one another's kittens, particularly if they all fall pregnant at similar times. They cooperate with each other and communally nurse the kittens and keep them clean. They will actively work together to guard the kittens against predators and invading tomcats. Even males living within a colony have been observed assisting with the rearing of kittens. They share food with them, groom them and even lie with them to keep them warm if the mother is away from the nest.

Opposite Kittens play to learn important survival skills and to help them bond with their sibling group. Their movements in play mimic many actions that will be needed later in life.

IT'S PLAYTIME!

As kittens grow up in the 'wild', it's essential that they learn to play because this helps them bond with their siblings and teaches them important survival skills needed for later life.

Kittens start to play when they are about two weeks of age, indulging in rough and tumble games in the nest. Once they have begun to walk, their behaviour mimics a jumbled version of postures and actions seen in the adult cat when hunting or fighting. They pounce, bite, kick and even walk sideways like a crab, with an arched back and tail. This is an invitation to play, often accompanied by a particular open-mouthed expression that is exclusively used at this time, to indicate that it's all in the name of fun. Kittens will often stop, cuddle up together and wash each other after an intense play fight of this kind.

They start to play with objects at about five weeks of age at the time when their mother is bringing live prey back to the nest. Only a week later these kittens may be killing prey of their own. Over the next couple of weeks they learn eye–paw coordination and the ability to manipulate small objects with ease, tossing them from one paw to the other. This will help them in later life to ensure that prey species are suitably dazed

As they get older, sibling play-fights can become more rough. This increase in aggression can serve as a cue for the mother to drive them from the nest.

before any attempt to kill them, as many are likely to bite back in self-defence. It pays to have a healthy respect for small rodents with sharp teeth!

Siblings will play with each other constantly until they are about 14 weeks old; many of the fights escalate as the kittens gets older and can become quite aggressive. Male kittens naturally play rougher games than females and this intense activity that continues for several months will motivate the mother to drive them away from the nest.

The success of predatory behaviour in adulthood in feral cats is not influenced by their quality of play as kittens. These skills are acquired by observing the mother and having access to plenty of prey at a young age. Most feral cats grow to become competent predators, albeit with particular personal preferences for the type of prey they pursue.

A CAT'S LICK AND A PROMISE

From the very day a kitten is born, grooming plays an important part in its life, as its mother washes her offspring to remove the placental sack, dry the fur and stimulate breathing.

By the third week of life a kitten can perform rudimentary grooming activity and three weeks later is regularly grooming itself and its siblings. Grooming cements the social bond between mother and kittens and can carry on into adulthood if the cats remain in the same colony. Mutual, or allogrooming, is focused predominantly around the head and ears, which is useful, as this is the area that a cat cannot reach with its own tongue. It also creates a communal scent that can be recognized on fellow members when they meet to help maintain the bond between them.

Cats can spend up to 30 per cent of their waking time grooming. Those areas around the head, ears and neck that can't be groomed directly using the tongue are washed by licking the paw and wiping it over the head, each paw cleaning one side in a series of sweeps from back to front.

But grooming is not just about keeping clean. It also acts to control temperature by spreading saliva onto the coat, which evaporates and cools the cat. Cats will always groom more in hot conditions or after hunting or playing. Licking and chewing at the coat, using the tiny incisor teeth at the

Cats wash hard-to-reach areas that can't be groomed directly by licking a paw and wiping it over the head in a series of sweeps from back-to-front .

front of the mouth, stimulates new hair growth and removes old hair, debris and parasites during the process. Licking also stimulates glands in the skin to keep the coat waterproof, essential for those cats forced to hunt in all weathers to survive.

In the cat's scent-focused world, grooming plays a dual role. By washing the inside of the hind legs and the lower abdomen from the anus outwards, scent is spread across the coat to reinforce the cat's own odour. After a cat has been in contact with any surfaces or brushed past something, it will stop and groom the area to restore its own smell and taste information about the objects it has encountered.

CAT NAPPING

When feral cats are not out and about hunting, patrolling or mating, they rest up. Cats can sleep, when they are well fed, for up to two-thirds of the day.

The amount of sleep that a feral cat has will vary according to the weather conditions, age (older cats and kittens sleep the most), hunger and sexual activity. If a cat is hungry and prey is scarce, it will be forced to rely on less sleep in order to survive.

Sleep is taken in a series of catnaps throughout the day. If the feral cat has the advantage of acquiring regular predictable food courtesy of a human carer, it will sleep for prolonged periods to preserve its energy. This is also a sensible strategy in social groups, as it avoids potential conflict that may come with more activity.

The place chosen to sleep will usually be hidden, dry and free from draughts. This den will change from time to time to ensure safety from predators and to prevent a build-up of parasites in the environment. The ambient temperature will dictate the posture that the cat will adopt while sleeping. Many climates will require the cat to maintain its body heat during sleep, so it will curl up its body with its nose tucked into the back leg and use its tail as a scarf wrapped around its head. Catnapping in the sun in the comparative safety of a colony may be done stretched out to gain the maximum benefit from the heat.

The depth of sleep varies, with the first 10–30 minutes of any bout being light, during which the cat will be easily woken. If the cat remains uninterrupted, with a full belly in a safe place, the sleep deepens and the body relaxes. During this time various muscles, maybe a paw or ear, will

Well-fed cats sleep for up to two-thirds of the day, usually in a series of cat naps. Studies of their brainwaves when sleeping deeply indicate that cats may dream as we do.

twitch and the eyes move under the eyelids. This period is referred to as paradoxical sleep, as the brainwaves show a similar pattern to the waking state. This is similar to the dreaming sleep of humans, so it's highly likely that cats dream too, but in their case probably of hunting or chasing birds!

CAT CHAT

Feral kittens naturally communicate vocally with their mothers, and sounds are also used by adult feral cats to greet each other in a social context, whether it's a friendly hello or a rebuff.

The sounds made can be grouped together according to how the mouth is used to create the sound. Those made by opening and then closing the mouth would relate to the 'miaow', with the 'm' sound formed before the mouth opens. Researchers have identified at least 19 different subtle

Sounds cats make when the mouth is fixed open are to do with aggression and defence. The noises used are intended to startle and thus enable escape.

Opposite House cats use vocal communication more often than feral cats.

variations of the 'miaow' that differ in volume, tone, intonation and pitch and in the situation in which they are used. In feral cats the 'miaow' sound is used by kittens to communicate with their mother, in social greeting between cats and in male and female 'calling' in preparation for mating.

The category of open/close mouth sounds also includes the harsher 'OW' call that occurs when a cat is in pain or extremely distressed. Feral cats use the 'miaow' relatively little in comparison to house cats and have no need for all the subtle sound variations that are produced by the pet cat to communicate with its owner. The feral cat relies heavily on non-verbal communication and signal, and will resort to sound only if they are unable to see the other cat or are involved in defensive or offensive displays of aggression.

The second group of sounds are made with the mouth shut, including the purr and the chirrup. The purr is predominantly used by kittens when suckling and in other situations between cats where positive social interaction is taking place or is desired. The chirrup is a greeting sound used between friendly, familiar cats when they meet each other after a period of absence.

The final category consists of those sounds made with the cat's mouth fixed open and these are focused exclusively on aggression and defence. These sounds include the hiss, snarl, growl, spit and shriek. The last is a particularly intense and effective noise used to startle an attacker enough to enable it to make its escape.

DID YOU KNOW…?

• *Research shows that cats purr at a frequency of vibration that aids bone and tissue growth and repair.*

• *According to research there are at least 19 'miaow' sounds differing in volume, tone, pitch and rhythm depending on the context in which they are used.*

• *Cats can also produce a 'silent miaow' which is considered to be a request for attention or a show of genuine affection from cat to owner. While the true meaning of the silent miaow is debateable it is probably a type of vocalization that produces a sound that is pitched too high for the human ear.*

The life and times of the domestic cat

The pet cat

Thousands of years ago the domestic cat started its relationship with humans. As our demands and lifestyles change, this relationship is now more complex and challenging than ever.

We now keep our cats predominantly for pleasure in towns and cities, with little need for them to perform their ancient and long-held role as rodent controllers.

Urban and suburban areas that contain cats, often several per household, do so at a population density far exceeding that which would occur naturally. Many owners now keep their pets exclusively indoors because they fear the risks of allowing them to roam freely in an environment full of potential danger. Even more alarmingly, cats are being bred with such extreme characteristics that owners are being advised to confine them for their own wellbeing. As the human population grows (at the current rate it will increase by 1 billion people every 11 years), the lifestyle of the cat is likely to become further restricted due to overcrowding.

Cats are being selectively bred to be 'dog-like', to be trainable and walk on a leash. We require them to adhere to strict house rules, yet they offer us unconditional love and attention. Are we in danger of losing sight of the inherent characteristics of the species that make it such a successful and unique animal?

Most of us still admire the qualities of the cat, despite the fact that they catch prey when they are well fed, scratch furniture and occasionally leave home if we dare to bring another cat into the household! Whatever lifestyle owners choose for their cats, there is no question that they are here to stay as a significant companion to humans in many parts of the world. We now invest a huge amount of time, emotion and money in our cats, and they are considered to be members of the family rather than just pets.

But the cat has had a chequered history in its association with humans, oscillating between the extremes of popularity and persecution in equal measures. Here is how it all happened…

THE DOMESTICATION STORY

The ancestor of today's felines, Pseudaelurus, evolved between 26 and 38 million years ago, but it has been a blink of an eye in comparison since cats and humans got together.

Prior to domestication, small wildcats were widely distributed throughout the world living self-sufficiently in parallel to man with little contact. There is some debate about the timing of the cat's domestication.

Originally, cats were domesticated for their ability to help with rodent control, but they were also widely deemed worthy of reverence with many gods in different cultures taking feline form.

Archeological findings in Cyprus of the remains of a human and an immature cat together potentially provide evidence dating back to 7500 BC. Statues from Turkey created around 6000 BC depict women playing with domesticated cats. However, genetic research published in 2007 claimed to prove that domestic cats derive from five founders from the Near East, now Iraq, Libya, Syria, Israel, Kuwait, south-eastern Turkey and south-western Iran, in the earliest agricultural Neolithic settlements that could have been in existence 100,000 years ago or more. The descendants of these five founders were then transported across the world with the help of humans.

TOP TEN CAT-OWNING COUNTRIES

Estimates for the global pet cat population vary widely, but figures quoted from 2006 make some staggering statistics:

USA	76,430,000	Italy	9,400,000
China	53,100,000	UK	7,700,000
Russia	12,700,000	Ukraine	7,350,000
Brazil	12,466,000	Japan	7,300,000
France	9,600,000	Germany	7,700,000

Whatever the accuracy of the timing, when traditional nomadic lifestyles came to an end, storage of crops became essential and the resulting grain stores attracted rodents. This in turn attracted the wildcat population of the area and they were encouraged to stay, certainly by the Egyptians, by feeding them scraps. The presence of an abundance of food, both scavenged and caught, with no predators or deterrence from people meant that colonies of cats soon formed. These cats resembled the African Wildcat seen today in the same region (*Felis silvestris lybica*), and even now they can be tamed if brought up from a kitten. Journeys across the Mediterranean enabled the cat to populate other continents. By the fourth century AD the cat's prowess as rodent deterrent had spread throughout the Roman Empire. In the 1700s cats were imported into the New World from Europe when colonies of settlers were overcome by plagues of rats.

Although cats were performing an important practical role for man, they were also seen as creatures worthy of some reverence and many gods took a feline form. For centuries cats were worshipped for their apparently supernatural powers. In Europe they developed a cult-like status and were used in various religious rituals. In medieval France cats were sacrificed to ensure a successful harvest and seen as the 'familiars' of witches.

The fall and rise of the cat

The initial reverence of cats then took a sinister twist and they began to be perceived as purely malevolent. The Catholic Church demonized cats in the 13th century and worship of cat-like gods was forbidden. The cat was considered the manifestation of the devil and hundreds of thousands of cats were tortured and killed, reducing the cat population of the time by over 90 per cent. Numbers were also affected by the plague, as many were culled due to the mistaken belief that they were carriers of the disease.

Cats were ritualistically slaughtered or casually tortured well into the 19th century in various parts of Europe until the Christian Churches finally stopped persecuting the so-called witches and their familiars. The expansion of towns and cities led to a high number of feral cats in Victorian Britain, far outnumbering the house cats of the period. However, by this time cats were becoming increasingly important household pets and in 1871 the first official cat show took place at the Crystal Palace in London, the organizers determined to change public perception of the cat. The trend caught on and the first cat show was organized on Broadway, New York, in 1881, with the first North American cat show held at the Madison Square Garden in 1895 with America's first cat show opened. By 1927 the Cats' Protection League was founded, solely to promote the welfare of cats in the UK. In 1866 the American Society for the Prevention of Cruelty to Animals (ASPCA) was founded. Once again the cat has renewed its popularity and continued to grow in status as the world's favourite pet.

Demonized until Victorian times by some Christian churches as a manifestation of the devil, the cat's place as an important household pet was finally acknowledged in 1871 when the first official cat show was held.

The impressive figures for the top ten cat-owning countries of the world on page 58 can only be considered as a rough guide, but it gives some insight into the scale of our enduring fascination for the feline species. Looking globally, it's easy to see that we are not alone in our love of cats, but all things considered, it's always *your very own cat* that's the focus of your love and attention.

In our pursuit of knowledge to understand our cats better, it's always good to start at the beginning and take some time to learn how each individual cat is created and how your very own cat came to have his unique personality.

Opposite There are only two basic coat colours in cats: black and red (or orange). All other colours are a variation of these. Eye colour is related to coat colour.

WHAT'S IN A CAT'S GENES?

In order to begin to appreciate the process involved in creating each individual cat, including your very own, you need to get acquainted with chromosomes and genes. So here comes the science lesson!

It all starts with a male and a female cat getting together and creating a new life that encompasses elements and characteristics of both parents. Each chromosome is made of protein and a single molecule of deoxyribonucleic acid (DNA) located inside the nucleus of animal and plant cells. Passed from parents to offspring, DNA contains the specific instructions that make each type of living creature unique. Chromosomes consist of long strands of genes and in each gene is information that guides development, growth and health. All the chromosomes in a cell are arranged in pairs (cats have 38 in total, while humans have 46). The two chromosomes in a pair have genes on them for the same characteristics. Therefore, a cat has two genes for every characteristic that it possesses.

When a sperm and egg join to form the first cell of a brand new kitten, half of each set of chromosomes from the male and female parent join to make a complete new set. This cell will duplicate to make billions of other cells containing the same genetic code that dictates what characteristics the kitten will have. How these traits are expressed will depend on how each parent's genes compete with each other for dominance. For example, some coat colours are dominant to others, so if one parent has a gene for a black coat and the other for a blue coat, the former will win out and the kitten will be born with a black coat.

Some genes are linked to the sex of the animal. A female has two of the same kind of sex chromosomes, XX, while the male has two different sex chromosomes, XY. The orange gene is on the X chromosome. This gene displays orange or black coat colour. A male with only one X chromosome can have only orange or

DID YOU KNOW...?

- *Eye colour is genetically related to coat colour.*

- *Cats with 'points', for example the Siamese, have a gene that limits the colour to the coolest parts of the cat's body at the head, tail and paws. As the cat gets older, and the blood flow decreases, the body starts to cool and the colour from the points starts to appear on the body.*

- *There are two basic colours of cats: black and red (also referred to as orange). All other colours are a variation of these.*

black, not both. If a male cat is both orange and black – a tortoiseshell or calico coat pattern – it must have all or part of both female X chromosomes. Male tortoiseshell or calico cats are therefore extremely rare and always sterile.

WHAT MAKES A CAT'S CHARACTER?

If a cat's appearance is dictated by its genes, then what about its individual personality? How much is your cat's personality influenced by nature (his genes) or nurture (his upbringing)?

There are numerous ways to categorize character and personality, but two basic models exist: your cat will either be excitable and reactive or slow and quiet. Variations in excitability and timidity are believed to be caused by inherited differences, such as the amount of adrenalin released when a cat faces a challenge. Certain breeds are described by temperament: Siamese are considered to be sociable, affectionate, sensitive and vocal; Burmese are assertive and outgoing; and the Persian is placid. This must imply that these characteristics are to some extent inherited.

Research into inheritability of temperament has examined the influence of the father on the personality of his offspring. This was thought to be a sound way to test genetic influence, as the father had no direct impact on the kittens' behaviour once they were born. The conclusion was that bold fathers produced bold kittens and timid fathers produced kittens of a similarly timid disposition. The mother may too have a similar genetic influence and the impact of her behaviour on her offspring at an early age would also have a profound effect. Kittens learn their responses to the environment and social situations by observing their mother.

Other more specific aspects of a cat's personality have been assessed in studies where subjective descriptions have been made of an individual cat's character. People were asked to confirm whether or not certain traits were present, some of which related specifically to a cat's response to other cats and humans, such as fearful, sociable, equable or hostile. Other observations included excitable, agile, curious, tense, vocal and watchful. This enabled researchers to establish human interpretation of fundamental elements of the cat personality. Subjective assessments of this kind can't produce hard and fast rules, but they do illustrate the

RELATIONSHIPS

I once followed the progress of Ragdoll siblings throughout their first year and their personalities ranged from shy to outgoing and from skittish to placid. As they grew, their characters were further shaped by their life experiences. One of the kittens went to live with a caring owner who, prior to a long plane journey that she was dreading, dutifully created a notebook containing all the details of her cat's likes and dislikes, habits and foibles. This would then be used in the unlikely event she should not return to ensure her Ragdoll was given the care he required. I have learnt over the years that precise descriptions of a cat's idiosyncrasies are irrelevant to future owners, as each human cat relationship is unique and understanding the fundamental characteristics of the individual and the species is all that is required for a happy life together.

complexity and diversity of a cat's characteristics. It's also only half the story, as learned behaviour and little quirks specific to one particular owner–cat relationship will add further dimensions to make each cat a unique individual.

Cats are not born with the ability to live alongside humans, so kittens need to develop positive associations with people and a home setting.

LEARNING TO LIVE WITH US

The domestic cat isn't born with the automatic ability to live in harmony with us humans; instead, cats have to *learn* to accept our very non-feline ways of living and behaving!

Your cat's personality, as discussed before, is influenced by inherited traits and the environment he's brought up in. Therefore, in order to ensure that your cat makes a good pet – and enjoys being one – it's important that he's provided with an upbringing full of positive associations with people and a home setting. A kitten's most significant behavioural and emotional

development takes place between two and seven weeks of age. This is referred to as 'the sensitive period', when kittens are particularly receptive to learning about their environment and other species. Anyone with a litter of kittens should take the opportunity to expose them to positive encounters with humans, dogs, other cats and any other domestic species during the first few weeks of life to give them every opportunity to form social bonds. This process is referred to as 'early socialization' and is very much the responsibility of the professional or hobby breeder.

Research conducted into the quality and quantity of handling during the sensitive period shows there are distinct benefits to providing the necessary socialization in the right way. The studies concluded that kittens that were handled by a number of different people during this crucial early period tended to be more sociable towards humans than those that didn't enjoy such handling. The mix of humans was also important, to include male and female, young and old.

But it's not just about people; kittens also need to understand what it's like to live in a domestic home. Positive exposure to environmental stimuli that would otherwise be challenging – noise, children, dogs, vacuum cleaners, different locations and even car journeys – equips the individual kitten with an understanding that these things are not to be feared.

Providing they are receiving the right socialization, kittens can ideally to go to their new homes when they are 12 weeks old. This enables them to spend as much time as possible with their mother and siblings first, from whom they can learn a great deal.

Opposite The 'sensitive period' between two and seven weeks of age is when kittens are particularly receptive to learning about their environment and other species.

PEDIGREE PERSONALITIES

Cats have been selectively bred since the late 1800s by enthusiasts keen to create exciting variations to the feline body shape, coat length and colour, and exhibit personality traits to go with their good looks.

There are now over 70 such registered breeds of cat worldwide. Feline personalities can vary dramatically, but generally the long-haired cats and the shorthair 'cobby' types, such as the British or American Shorthair, tend to be referred to as 'laid-back' and 'placid', while the lean Oriental types are more outgoing.

Personality is acquired through a complex interplay of hormones, genetics and early experiences, so it's impossible to say that any two cats,

Opposite Siamese are sociable, playful cats that dislike being left on their own. They can form bonds with other cats and are also vocal.

irrespective of their breeding, will behave in exactly the same way or grow up to have identical traits. However, describing each breed by its behaviour gives a rule-of-thumb insight into characteristics that may dictate how suitable a particular breed is for a prospective owner's environment and lifestyle. Some qualities of temperament, such as 'lively' or 'highly sociable', may not suit a person who spends long hours at work, as the needs of this particular cat for company and entertainment will exceed what such an owner can offer in practical terms. If, on the other hand, a breed is described as 'shy' and 'sensitive', it may not be the ideal pet for someone with a hectic lifestyle and unpredictable routines.

So, researching pedigrees before purchasing is important, as not all types of cat are bound to be compatible with all kinds of owner. A cat is a serious commitment and a potential companion for over 20 years. Therefore, getting it wrong at the start is a potential recipe for an unhappy cat *and* owner. So try before you buy!

PICKING A PEDIGREE

Which breed would most suit your personality? These are currently the most popular breeds worldwide, with a few hints on what to expect if you decide to share your home with a pedigree cat.

British/American Shorthair

This is a friendly yet undemanding, placid and gentle cat that enjoys human company, but prefers to sit near you rather than on your lap.

Birman

This is a gentle and quiet cat that makes a good family pet, as it loves to be with people.

Siamese

An intelligent, sensitive and vocal cat. Siamese are playful and often described as 'dog-like', as they love company and hate to be left alone. They can form strong bonds with other cats, mainly Siamese. They are also very talkative!

Persian

These are gentle and often undemanding cats, but they are the high-maintenance divas of the cat world, requiring daily grooming to keep their long coats in good condition.

Burmese

These cats are often described as 'more like a dog', as they are outgoing and energetic. They are vocal and love human attention, but can get up to mischief when they are bored or left alone for long periods. Like the Bengal, they can also be very territorial.

Ragdoll

This is a placid and gentle cat that's content with human company without making too many demands for attention. Its coat needs grooming, but it isn't quite as long and prone to knots as that of the Persian.

Maine Coon

Gentle giants, Maine Coons are affectionate and relaxed yet outgoing and great with people. But don't expect their voice to be as big as their body size, as they produce a quiet chirping sound to communicate.

Norwegian Forest Cat

A slightly smaller cat than the Maine Coon, the Norwegian Forest Cat is relaxed, confident and sociable, with a love for the outdoor life.

Oriental Shorthair

This cat is very similar to the Siamese in temperament: loyal, affectionate, vocal and demanding!

Bengal

The Bengal was originally created as a hybridization between the Asian Leopard and a domestic cat. The first few generations of the Bengal, referred to as F1, F2 and F3, are very shy, but subsequent generations have become playful, active and vocal pets that love water. They are very strong, muscular cats and they can be highly territorial.

DID YOU KNOW...?

- *Siamese kittens are born white and their points change to darker fur when they are about four weeks old.*

- *A kitten's ability to perceive pain is present at birth.*

- *Normal kittens have a heart rate of over 200 beats per minute.*

- *Kittens will suckle from a non-lactating female given the opportunity as well as a lactating one until they are three weeks old, showing that the reward of milk is not necessary to initiate or maintain suckling behaviour.*

INSIDE A KITTEN'S LIFE

Kittens develop rapidly from birth, both physically and emotionally, but during the first two weeks of life their responses remain limited and they are completely dependent on their mother for their survival.

Kittens are born without sight or hearing and they use touch, scent and the sensation of warmth to locate the mother's teat to feed. Urination and defecation are stimulated by their mother by licking the kitten's anus. At this age kittens are relatively immobile and they use a slow paddling movement to travel very short distances within the nest area. During the first two weeks of life their eyes will open and their teeth start to grow.

During the third and fourth week the kittens' eyesight starts to guide them towards their mother rather than relying on her warmth and smell alone. A rudimentary form of walking emerges during the third week and by four weeks of age the kittens can move a reasonable distance away from the nest. They can now use the feline's famed body-righting reflex to turn in midair to land on their feet if they fall. At four weeks of age kittens would normally commence the weaning process from their mother's milk to solid food provided by their owners.

By the fifth week kittens can run in short bursts and by six weeks of age they have acquired all the basic movements of an adult cat. As weaning progresses, kittens become increasingly responsible for initiating bouts of nursing, many of which will be rejected by the mother. By this time

Weaning from their mother's milk onto solid food normally begins when the kittens are about four weeks of age.

CALCULATING YOUR CAT'S AGE

cat age	equivalent in human years	cat age	equivalent in human years
1	15	13	68
2	24	14	72
3	28	15	76
4	32	16	80
5	36	17	84
6	40	18	88
7	44	19	92
8	48	20	96
9	52	21	100
10	56	22	104
11	60	23	108
12	64	24	112

Rate of ageing in cats

Cats age at a different rate to humans, but it's useful to calculate how old your cat is in equivalent terms. The basic rule is that one cat year is equal to four human years, but the first two years of a cat's life progress slightly differently. The first month is equivalent to the first year of a baby's life, and by the time a kitten is three months old it would be the equivalent of a four-year-old toddler. A six-month-old cat equates to a ten-year-old child and a one year-old cat year is equivalent to a 15-year-old human adolescent.

COMING OF AGE

The true characteristics of your cat will reveal themselves at the stage of reaching social maturity, when as an individual he understands his territorial needs and role in relation to other cats.

Your cat will usually become socially mature between the ages of 18 months and four years, on average at the age of two. He is now fully grown (some of the larger breeds like the Maine Coon can keep growing until they are four years old) and his personality as an individual is established.

This is a time when there may well be subtle shifts in the way that your cat sees the world. Disputes with other cats outside may take on a more

serious note, or he may even start to feel the pressure of establishing territory in the face of such opposition. Relationships with other cats in the same household will change as they start to see each other as rivals rather than playmates. This transition happens gradually and is rarely something that you as owner will recognize. Cats with previously close relationships that slept together or groomed each other will cool off and be found in different parts of the house, rather than curled up in one cosy bed. They may stop playing together or the play fighting may escalate into something more aggressive, with neither cat backing down as each one attempts to establish their ability to win an argument. Most cats in a multi-cat household will agree to disagree and create their own personal dens or core areas within the home where they feel safe and are free from invasion by others. The home then gets divided up and the cats timeshare the space as if they were separate individuals with overlapping territories.

As cats in the same household reach maturity they may stop playing together and attempt to claim their own territories within their shared space.

to work their relationship with their owners and specific communication will take place between you and your cat. By now you will have discovered what your cat likes and how he shows that he wants it. The training programme will be well on its way to completion and, probably without you realizing it, your cat will be firmly in the driving seat of the relationship by now!

Health issues may also be significant at this time of life for the pedigrees. As breeding for specific traits involves a disproportionately small 'gene pool', the pedigree cat is more prone to inheritable diseases than the average domestic 'moggy'. These diseases, such as heart or kidney problems, often become evident as a young adult.

Cats of this age have stopped growing and have usually, unless required for breeding, been neutered. Both these physiological changes will lead to a significant reduction in your cat's energy requirements. If his previous calorific intake is maintained and combined with a more sedentary lifestyle, weight gain is almost inevitable.

THE MID-LIFE CRISIS

It pays to monitor your cat's behaviour as he approaches middle age, usually between six and eight years of age, in order to identify situations that could result in problems brewing for the future.

If your cat is going outside less frequently, for example, it could indicate that he's finding it difficult establishing his 'rights of passage' through the territory outside. As his owner, you provide your cat with a strong feeling of security, so if he's only going out when you are there, it may well be a sign that there are underlying problems. If this is combined with your cat's sudden disinterest in play, then alarm bells should start to ring.

A reduction in the intensity of play once a cat has matured is extremely common and almost inevitable, but to stop completely is a bad sign. Play is a natural leisure activity, so should be ongoing for a lifetime. Any lack of interest may be as a direct consequence of you the owner initiating fewer games. However, if you are still taking as active a part in play as ever but your cat is less willing, then the root of the problem may be pressure from other cats. If a cat feels threatened or intimidated in any way by the presence of others, then play is one of the first activities that stops, as it's impossible to maintain vigilance against possible attack when lost in the excitement of a game. Sadly, the enemy may be *inside* the home, in that a competitive cat in a household may claim toys as an important resource and a less assertive individual will feel unable to indulge in a game if the competitive cat is around.

There may be more cats outside or they may just be encroaching further into your cat's territory as he fails to establish his own boundaries. Some cats, under overwhelming pressure from others outside, can even decide to remain housebound rather than risk attack.

If your cat seems disinclined to venture outside, he may have territorial issues keeping him housebound. These may arise from competition with fellow pets.

If your cat is kept indoors or is less inclined to exercise outside, then middle age is the time to step up the entertainment. See pages 116–117 for how to stimulate and excite your cat with the right toys and games.

THE MATURE CAT

It's difficult to accurately assess a cat's age unless they are very young or very old, and many a mature cat will be hard to distinguish from a young adult.

A cat is considered mature between the ages of seven and ten years. How your cat looks and how his body responds to the passing of time at this life stage will depend on his genetics, lifestyle, nutrition and general health. However, this is the time when potentially age-related disease may become evident.

As your cat becomes mature, he will have mastered the relationship with you as his owner completely and start to use more vocalization to communicate his needs. As cats don't use a great deal of sound naturally in social situations (see page 52), the increase in a variety of 'miaow' sounds is tailored specifically to get *you* to provide specific services.

By this time your cat may well have moved home several times and even had to deal with the introduction of another cat into the household. Many multi-cat households are the product of a series of acquisitions rather than cats brought up together, so mature cats may well have had to deal with this experience at least once by the time they are ten.

This is also a time of life when your cat can get set in his ways and any challenges he faces may be dealt with by a strategy of avoidance rather than confrontation, causing a general lack of activity and a 'couch potato' lifestyle. This can lead to gradual weight gain over a period of time, and if it has been creeping up for a few years and it wasn't addressed when he was younger, then the mature life stage is when obesity starts to have an impact on your cat's health (see pages 173–176). Weight isn't the primary measure of obesity, as cats have different frame sizes and their optimum weight will differ accordingly. A body condition 'scoring' system has been developed that judges a cat's silhouette from two different aspects. Ideally, your cat should narrow at the waist when viewed from above and his ribs should be easily felt but not clearly visible.

THE AGEING CAT

Your cat will be approaching his senior years at the age of 11 and from 15 years old onwards a cat is advanced enough in age to be referred to as geriatric.

General physical changes take place during these two late stages of life that reflect the overall ageing process. Your cat's fur starts to lose its shine, his skin becomes less elastic and his coat colour may fade from jet black to brown or white hairs appear. Hearing and sight deteriorate and, if severely affected, your cat may appear less responsive and more withdrawn. He may even lose his appetite as his ability to smell and taste food declines. Cats normally have a poor motivation to drink, but this also becomes more noticeable as they age and they can become permanently dehydrated, leading to uncomfortable chronic constipation. Sleep increases and

CATS HAVE SLAVES!

Carol and I were deep in conversation when her elderly cat, China, walked into the room and made a small squeaking sound. Carol immediately rose from her chair, went to the kitchen and poured some cat milk into a saucer and gave it to China. She returned and we continued our chat until China approached his owner again, making a deeper more insistent noise whereupon Carol reached for the brush and absentmindedly started smoothing China's slightly dishevelled coat. When China made yet another sound shortly afterwards I had to ask Carol whether or not I was correct in presuming that each noise represented a particular demand. In response she informed me that China did indeed have about twelve different demands developed over a long and happy relationship of fifteen years that included 'open the door', 'carry me', 'play with me' and others that I witnessed during my visit. Smart but not unique as many owners of elderly cats will know!

Elderly cats sleep more, sometimes for up to 18 hours a day.

out as the muscles that keep them sheathed weaken, so they need regular trimming to avoid getting caught or growing into the pad.

Changing behaviour

All the potential physical deterioration associated with old age will also have an impact on your cat's routines and general behaviour: old cats tend to go outdoors and hunt less, and fill the consequent void in activity with increased sleep, sometimes for as much as 18 hours or more a day. They may play and groom less, and even have 'accidents' in the house if they forget acceptable toilet habits.

However, it's not all doom and gloom for you and your senior cat. Spending many years with your cat allows a relationship to develop so familiar that it creates a depth of understanding between the two of you that's difficult to reproduce in a shorter time scale. Your senior cat will tend to vocalize more as he learns to 'talk' to get what he wants from you; in turn, you learn to interpret each subtle nuance of sound and understand what is being requested. Cats in old age also turn to humans for affection and reassurance, and previously aloof or unsociable cats can become uncharacteristically loving in later life.

SENIOR SCENARIOS

Old age is not a disease in itself, but it does require an extra degree of care from you as a loving owner to make life as comfortable as possible for your elderly companion.

Regular annual health checks are a must for the senior cat and your vet may even recommend six-monthly examinations if your cat copes well with surgery visits.

Cats cannot regulate their body temperature when they are older. It's therefore important that you offer a number of warm beds that are easily accessible and away from draughts. Make sure that the bed is thick with fleeces, blankets or similar material to prevent any sores developing over any prominent bones. Some older cats find curling up a little tricky, particularly if they are arthritic and stiff, so provide a bed that is big enough for your cat to stretch out to give him added comfort.

Older cats may be less agile than they used to be, but regular activity will help to retain muscle mass and aid circulation. Gentle and regular playtime for short periods is recommended for the elderly. Cat flaps can be a problem if your elderly cat is stiff or arthritic and this alone may put him off going outside for fresh air. You may want to go out with him to walk around the garden, giving him the exercise he needs and the company to make him feel more secure. Climbing may also be a problem for your elderly cat and favoured resting places may be inaccessible unless you provide graduated steps for him, such as footstools and boxes.

Any loss of appetite can be stimulated by warming food to room temperature to release more odour, as smell is so important in stimulating a cat's appetite. If your cat appears to be exhibiting signs of senility (see panel opposite), providing environmental stimulation in the form of hunting and foraging games and structured interaction can lead to an increase in his cognitive function and a better quality of life.

SIGNS OF SENILITY

These include:

- *A change in the sleep–wake cycle*
- *Excessive vocalization*
- *Decreased appetite and grooming*
- *Disorientation or confusion*
- *Breakdown of toilet training*
- *Staring into corners, repetitive pacing*

Households with
more than one cat
must have sufficient
resources to fulfil the
needs of all the cats.
Tensions may
nevertheless arise,
particularly where
one cat is timid and
another more bold.

The right mix

Multi-cat households will work best when you take care to combine the appropriate individuals in an environment that offers enough resources to fulfil all the needs of each cat. Some cats are better suited to social living than others, but unfortunately it's difficult to determine this at a young age. Littermates of the opposite sex would seem the most sensible option, providing you have seen them playing with each other and obviously enjoying one another's company. A combination of one extremely confident and bold kitten and a timid, shy one could well lead to bullying and intimidation as adults.

Another potential problem relates to those owners who decide to keep kittens from their own female's litter. The female cat produces hormones during pregnancy and gestation that programme her to care for her young in such a way as to maximize the chance of their survival. Once those kittens are weaned and the associated hormone drive to behave in a certain way is no longer present, a very different relationship often develops. It would not be a healthy strategy to encourage male offspring to remain close, and females are potential competitors for mating, so it's probably not surprising that tensions can occur once the kittens are five or six months old.

Mistakes are often made when cats are added to harmonious and stable social groups. Most groups actively resist the introduction of strangers, particularly if the newcomer is an adult. The resulting tension can even cause cracks in an otherwise positive relationship between a group of established cats. But there are some particularly equable cats that are supremely suited to communal living, mixing with all other members of the household and single-handedly establishing the group scent that binds the individuals together as a group.

THE ENEMY OUTSIDE

It's easy to overlook pressures from outside having a direct effect on your multi-cat household, but for those cats with access outdoors it can mean all the difference between living in harmony or disharmony.

If one of your cats experiences a constant threat of danger from invading cats in the territory, he will react by assuming a state of persistent heightened arousal that impacts on his mood and therefore behaviour and attitude towards his fellow felines in the home. Take away those pressures and the same cats may cohabit in a perfectly amicable way.

Even indoor cats are not immune from the pressure of the great outdoors, as strange cats can easily be viewed in the garden through windows and full-length glass or patio doors. The glass offers no sense of protection for the resident cat; spotting such an obvious threat causes the body to pump adrenalin in order to prepare for a fight. Unfortunately, it may well be the companion cat or cats indoors that become the innocent victims of the ensuing aggression, as the intense emotional response to the perceived danger outdoors can easily get re-directed onto the wrong target (see page 136).

Owners of multiple cats are dedicated cat lovers and strays often gravitate towards them like moths to a flame. This is for two reasons: first, people in the neighbourhood will know about their enthusiasm for cats and make sure that they are the first to be told about any local strays, and second, the cats will gravitate towards an environment that is rich in food, shelter and all things cat-friendly. A hungry stray will try very hard to move in with a group that enjoys the plentiful source of food that multi-cat owners provide. Their behaviour is often wily to the extreme as they approach and make themselves known to you, appearing gentle and passive. They offer no aggression towards your resident cats, but equally show no signs of timidity or weakness that could potentially cause them to drive it away. Once you decide the cat can stay as it seems to get on well with yours, it will, once established, make it a mission to intimidate and remove the others and claim the place as its own. Be warned!

GOLDFISH BOWL

Poor Gyro, a Siamese, was particularly perturbed when his owners demolished the back wall of their kitchen and replaced it with, for want of a better description, a large glass 'box'. Gyro's response was to spray small squirts of pungent urine against the glass at every opportunity. Cats need to be camouflaged from the outside world and large expanses of glass can be stressful as they offer nowhere to hide when viewing the great outdoors. Pet behaviourists refer to this as 'the goldfish bowl effect' as cats can feel very exposed and vulnerable. The strategic placing of furniture and a sheet of self-adhesive opaque film on the lower section of the glass soon restored Gyro's sense of security and his behaviour returned to normal.

The secret of a happy cat

Being cat-friendly

Almost any home can be made cat-friendly with a little imagination, but the secret of a happy cat is not just about the environment – it's also about how you interact with your cat.

We have looked inside the cat to see how it works, studied its behaviour in the wild and explored its origins as a pet and life stages. All of this information provides part of the answer to the ultimate question: what makes a cat happy?

Now it's time to focus specifically on the cat or cats with which you share your home and put the knowledge gleaned in the previous three sections to good use. We all wish for our cats to be as happy as possible and we know that their happiness is influenced greatly by how we behave and what kind of lifestyle we offer them when they share our homes. This section is devoted to ensuring that you provide the best possible environment to cater for your cat's needs and general entertainment. Getting the home right for your cat by providing the right equipment and facilities is important, particularly if you keep your cat exclusively indoors. Your cat's ability to choose, based on personal likes and dislikes, is severely curtailed when you are in sole charge of making the decisions. If you base those decisions on purely human considerations or what *you* perceive to be important to your cat, then you could be making life a little less than perfect for the family's feline.

Providing the appropriate mix of food, shelter, love and entertainment is the key to catering for your cat's needs and making him a happy cat.

As the cat has such specific needs, it isn't enough *just* to provide some food, shelter and love. While these elements are as important as ever to the pet cat, it's the quality and quantity of each that is the key. There are practical challenges about the provisions you make for your cat in the home. How many cat beds should you provide? Where should you locate the scratching posts? What games should you play? What's more, there are even emotional questions that need to be answered. Exactly how *much love* should you give?

The decisions and choices you make throughout your cat-owning life are pivotal to your cat's wellbeing. I will therefore endeavour to show you how to keep your cat happy by making the right choices.

The decisions and choices you make in your cat-owning life are pivotal to his wellbeing. It is important to take account of the cat's perspective as well as your own human considerations.

THE RIGHT RELATIONSHIP

The modern owner–cat relationship is a complex one. While it isn't a bad thing that you should care greatly for your feline companion, it's important to maintain a healthy balance.

Many people see their pets as members of the family, and as a result they put their cat's wellbeing in making decisions about, for instance, holidays and moving house at their very centre. However, pet ownership should be about mutual benefit and pleasure for *both* parties.

When it comes to viewing the relationship from a cat's perspective, it's probably right to presume that cats see us as equals, socially, rather than anything to be revered or obeyed! Their behaviour, however, will change depending on their mood or the circumstances, and they will oscillate between kitten, juvenile and adult responses during interaction with their owners. You may also observe, if you have more than one cat, that they can be competitive and view you more as a resource than a companion when it comes to allowing other cats to have access.

A healthy relationship between you and your cat allows each of you to have a life outside of it. Too much attention and too much time in each other's company can create a dependency where your cat feels unable to do anything without your emotional support. Cats in this situation can become deeply distressed when their owners are absent and some even develop stress-related illness. This kind of intensity doesn't make you or your cat truly happy.

Cats should be allowed to be cats and, to a certain extent, to dictate the quality and quantity of interaction with their owners. Spending at least part of the day in normal cat activity keeps the feline spirit alive, so encouraging your cat to play, explore, climb and jump on a daily basis is a beneficial routine to adopt.

TALKING IN CAT

We all feel we have a special insight into our own cat's mind, but are we really communicating with them? Do they understand what we are saying to them and vice versa?

The beauty of the owner–cat relationship is that it can function fairly well without a common language. Your cat may signal a specific demand and you may well misinterpret the communication as a request for something completely different and respond accordingly, yet it never really seems to matter. If owners appear compliant, then their cats will keep trying until they get their message across. They are very tolerant of our lack of understanding!

Cats communicate with each other when they are face to face by using combinations of body posture, movement and ear, head and tail carriage. Some of their body language is very descriptive, but other signals involve such subtle shifts that humans can easily miss them. This makes cats particularly adept at reading non-verbal cues, which seems to apply to their relationship with their owners. If you communicate something to your cat and you don't, in your heart of hearts, *really* mean it, then your cat will know you are faking it. Cats will always know when you are scared or angry despite how hard you try to hide it, because subtle changes in your body language will give your true feelings away.

This leads to, arguably, the first rule of communication with your cat: he will always know your true intentions and mood, so don't even bother to pretend. Remember this the next time you approach your cat, just like normal, with a worming pill hidden in your pocket. Your cat will know because you will reveal your intentions in the way you behave. The secret is to convince yourself that all is well and you will appear relaxed and much less threatening.

Cats communicate through movement, body posture and ear, head and tail carriage, and are extremely adept at reading non-verbal clues coming from their owners.

Conversely, you need to learn how to interpret the subtle nuances of your cat's behaviour. Cats do everything for a reason; every move and posture is there for a purpose no matter how nonchalant they may appear at first sight. Next time your cat approaches you, or draws your attention towards him, try to 'think cat' before you presume you know what's on his mind.

Cats do everything for a reason, so any change in posture potentially conveys a message. Every time he approaches you, try to 'think cat' to tell what he wants.

WHAT HE WANTS FROM YOU

Contrary to popular opinion, cats don't always want food or petting when they approach their owners. This misunderstanding can lead to frustrated, overweight cats that can't see why they are unable to communicate.

Cats will use vocalization for several reasons: to greet their owners after a period of absence, communicate mood, alert their owner to danger or to request something. Your cat can also use sound as a warning to deter you from doing something he doesn't like. When your cat returns from outdoors, he may use a particular cry to indicate that he has brought prey back to the den. He will use a chirruped greeting if you have been out or he has returned from a garden excursion. It's a brief sound that requires an equally short acknowledgement, which depending on your cat's personality can be anything from a brief verbal 'reply' to a 'pick up and cuddle'. If you are unclear which your cat would prefer, struggling away from you is a good indication that he would rather not be picked up!

The use of vocalization by cats is a learned behaviour, as sound is almost always reinforced by attentive owners, so therefore cats are encouraged to repeat it. Some cats use very similar sounds for all demands, but give some intention of their desires by standing near the object in question, such as a door or food cupboard, while staring directly at their owner or the object. An alert to danger, for example, is often accompanied by pacing, particularly from one window to another because the perceived threat has been detected outside. Restlessness accompanied by vocalization prior to using a litter tray may indicate your cat is not satisfied with the facilities.

Play mimics the behaviours associated with hunting and is naturally rewarding – it seems the more he plays, the more he will want to play.

Opposite Cats of all ages should be encouraged to play for the benefits of exercise and general stimulation. Middle-aged spread can be addressed by exercise through play.

Rubbing is a marking behaviour that your cat will commonly perform on your legs when greeting you or waiting for you to feed him. You don't need to acknowledge this action specifically; owners frequently find it confusing that their cat appears to solicit their attention in this way and then reject it when they bend down to stroke.

If your cat falls over in front of you to expose his belly, you may well misinterpret this as him wanting his stomach rubbed. But it actually indicates your cat's sense of security in your presence, so an outstretched hand towards his most vulnerable area will often be greeted with a grab, kick and bite!

A CAT'S KIND OF LOVING

Owners tend to feel that love is only expressed by showing tactile affection. But unfortunately holding and caressing for all but the most socialized and tolerant cats is often regarded as restrictive and controlling.

If you want to create a positive feeling in your cat when you walk into a room, then playtime is a good tool to increase the bond. Play, as previously discussed, is an enjoyable activity for your cat. It mimics the behaviour associated with hunting and predatory sequences that are hard-wired in your cat's brain and naturally rewarding. It's also exercise that seems to have a cumulative effect: the more your cat has, the more he enjoys it and the more he wants!

Cats of any age should be encouraged to play for the benefits of exercise and general stimulation. Kittens show optimum development and become well-rounded adults if they experience all kinds of play and games as youngsters. Old cats with active brains excited through play will enjoy a slowing down of the progression of senile changes as their years advance. Obesity and the almost inevitable middle-aged spread can also be addressed by regular exercise through play.

Busy owners often include play with their cats in their schedule at random times of the day when the thought and inclination arise. This will not be the ideal time for the cat, as being creatures that thrive on routine they will undoubtedly have patterns of activity that span a 24-hour period with little major deviation. It's unlikely that your cat will have any desire to play in the mid-afternoon if this period is normally set aside for sleep or rest. However, if he has a mad half an hour dashing round the house at nine o'clock at night, this would be the time to consider a scheduled game or two.

Playtime doesn't have to be prolonged and actually has the most beneficial effects if it's provided relatively frequently in short, energetic bursts of activity. Six exciting five-minute sessions with a toy on the end of a rod and string is worth much more than a solid 30 minutes waggling a fabric mouse in front of a bored cat's nose!

THE FELINE-FRIENDLY HOME

A home that appeals to your cat doesn't have to look like a zoo enclosure, but there are perfect compromises that can be made that will enable you and him to cohabit in comfort.

If you are a lover of contemporary minimalist interiors, you are probably going to have to adjust more than most to provide everything your cat needs. Open-plan living spaces with clean lines and an overall lack of clutter is the basis of the modern style, but this couldn't be further removed from a cat's natural habitat. Although the domestic cat is highly adaptable to most landscapes, it still requires a degree of camouflage to enable it to roam relatively inconspicuously. This camouflage can be found almost anywhere apart from the contemporary living space; it's very hard to disguise a cat in an empty room! Your cat thinks it's a tabby (probably most think they are tigers), and standing behind a few blades of grass or a chair is all he needs to feel safe and disguised enough to remain undetected.

The cluttered home provides a haven of possibilities for a cat, offering high perches and plenty of places to disappear from view. Taking time out from social demands is an essential part of everyday life for a cat, so private places and secret hideaways are an important facility. Make his refuge a warm one too, like the bottom of the airing cupboard, and you are talking five-star accommodation!

It's hard to beat a staircase in a home, as this gives your cat access to high platforms – which is probably how our cats see the space 'upstairs' – and represents what he perceives as a place of safety. If your property is single storey, then your cat's instinctive need to jump up high when in danger has to be fulfilled with shelving, cupboards or other possible platforms.

Every room within the home and every type of dwelling has specific considerations, so it's worth assessing your living space, one area at a time, to ensure that there is at least one small allowance made for your feline family member.

THE FELINE-FRIENDLY KITCHEN

The kitchen is a key area in the home, as it's often where many of the cat's resources are located, but it's also one that poses potential security threats and health hazards for your feline.

Opposite Cats have an instinctive need to jump up high when in danger, so they like staircases. They provide high platforms and represent what they perceive as a place of safety.

Opposite In the kitchen, locate your cat's food as far away from entry and exit points as possible, preferably in a place that can't be viewed from outside.

Cat flaps, windows for entry and exit, food and water bowls, litter trays and beds are frequently placed for convenience in the kitchen or in utility areas adjacent to it. This all makes the room an important area, but also one of the most vulnerable to attack from other cats outside, lured in by the promise of food.

But with a little careful planning you can increase your cat's sense of safety by locating the food as far away from the entry and exit point as possible. If your cat is kept indoors, then he still runs the risk of seeing other cats through the windows, so locating important resources such as litter trays, food and water away from areas that are easily viewed from the outside will make him feel more comfortable and secure.

The kitchen can also be a place of potential hazards, so it's worth doing a quick safety check to make sure that your cat won't come to any harm – see the panel above.

Cats like to move about on high surfaces and they will, if allowed, walk across work surfaces in the kitchen where food is prepared, particularly if it gives them access to a window and the view outside. Any punishment to deter your cat from using the surfaces will only result in him walking on them when you are not there, so you need to try an alternative strategy. Fit a sheet of heavy paper to your food preparation surfaces and fix it in place using heavy objects or a removable mastic adhesive. Stick strips of double-sided adhesive tape in a criss-cross pattern over the upper surface of the paper. Choose a low-tack stationery tape that only feels slightly sticky. If your cat jumps up, he will feel an unpleasant tacky sensation on his paws and this may well deter him from going there again.

THE FELINE-FRIENDLY LIVING ROOM

Your cat will undoubtedly want to share quality time with you in this room of recreation, but there may be things that you can do to make it feel that much more attractive to him.

The main living area of your home is a place where you enjoy your rest and relaxation time. It's often the focus for entertaining friends, watching

Windows are good for seeing what is going on outside, but cats prefer smaller windows in darker rooms since these provide camouflage so they feel less vulnerable.

Opposite Your bed offers the ultimate in warmth and security to your cat: it is a raised platform covered in soft bedding and it smells of you.

television and generally chilling after a hard day. Some television programmes can be interesting to your cat, but don't presume that everything you watch will be equally enthralling for him. Cats do respond to shapes on the screen that move like prey animals and are often very interested in the squeaks and tweets of wildlife documentaries. Dedicated cat DVDs have been produced that put together a sequence of all the sights and sounds that attract cats, to appeal to the housebound, but these shouldn't be relied upon as a sole source of entertainment.

Windows are a significant viewing point for the great outdoors, but, contrary to most people's understanding, cats usually prefer smaller windows in darker rooms if given the choice. Large expanses of glass appear to be confusing to cats. They see the garden or the street outside and all the potential dangers that they harbour, but fail to grasp that they are safe indoors. It all comes down to camouflage. Glass doesn't give your cat any opportunity for concealment while he checks out the territory, and if it's a full-length window or patio door, then the ultimate horror may occur and he may come face to face with next-door's tomcat on the other side.

Sheets of decorative static film can be attached to the lower portion of full-length glass that opaque the view yet still enable the room to remain light. To your cat this will look like a more solid defence. In conjunction with this strategy, you can ensure that he has a high perch somewhere near the window from which he can view the outdoors in a position of authority. If you don't fancy putting any film over a full-length window, then the strategic positioning of potted house plants near the glass may provide just enough camouflage for your cat to feel a little safer.

THE FELINE-FRIENDLY BEDROOM

Your bedroom is potentially the ultimate delight for your cat. It will probably be upstairs if you have more than one storey, and therefore perceived as safe, as he has to 'climb' to get there.

It will also be the place that offers the warmth of a duvet or bedding on a raised platform, again allowing your cat to go 'up' to sleep, *and* it smells strongly of you. This provides a tremendous sense of security and enables your cat to sleep deeply in the knowledge that he is safe. If he has the added privilege of being allowed on the bed when you are there, it further reinforces the bedroom as his favourite resting place.

This can create problems, however, if the regime needs to change for whatever reason: a new baby or partner, for example, may make it impractical for your cat to continue to sleep with you. Changing the routine and depriving your cat of such a huge perk can frustrate or even depress him.

Achieving a compatible sleep–wake cycle can also be challenging in a species that is more naturally active during the hours of darkness. Some cats find it impossible to sleep quietly beside their owners and can indulge in mischievous play activity at 4 am that usually includes bouncing off human heads! If this has happened to you, then don't employ tactics to avoid too much disturbance, such as getting up to let him out, feeding him or playing downstairs to avoid waking your partner. This merely acts as an excellent reward for the behaviour and consequently it will be a difficult habit to break. Creating the rule that you and your cat sleep separately in the first place usually prevents these kinds of problems from occurring.

If the master bedroom does become such an important resource, it can also be a place of conflict in multi-cat households, as individuals compete for the best spot. Providing heated pads or raised cat beds in

Opposite If your gardens contains everything your cat needs, he is less likely to roam in search of what he is looking for.

other bedrooms or even allocating space in your own room for such additions may go some way to finding a sensible compromise. The most important rule of all is not to respond to attention-seeking behaviour at night, otherwise it will become impossible to stop.

THE FELINE-FRIENDLY OUTDOORS

If your cat is able to access your garden, it's wise to ensure that everything he needs is contained within it. Cats are not restricted by boundaries and will roam to find what they require.

Having a cat-friendly garden won't *guarantee* that your cat stays put, but it *may* make a difference. As your cat leaves the house, he will need to check

that all is well in the territory and that he is free from danger. The more confident cat may stride boldly from the house, but many prefer to be more cautious in their approach. This process of checking and assessing potential danger is best carried out with a degree of camouflage so that he can observe without being seen. Camouflage can be provided by the strategic placement of shrubs in patio pots, garden furniture or mature borders. All-year-round protection can be guaranteed by ensuring that a proportion of the planting is evergreen.

High vantage points to observe the territory from a safe location are plentiful in gardens with garages, sheds, fences and trees, all offering opportunities to catch some rays and check out the local competition. Unfortunately, these will also be popular with the rest of the local feline population, meaning that your cat may not be the sole occupier of the shed roof.

Cats often seek out the boundaries of their territory for latrine sites, but under pressure from a densely populated neighbourhood, they may well use locations as near as possible to the relative safety of the home. This might be the first patch of gravel or soil outside the back door. Providing your cat with an attractive purpose-made toilet area is an effective solution – see the panel above.

Opposite Most cats prefer to be cautious as they approach the outside, checking for potential dangers from a vantage point where they can see but not be seen, such as behind patio pots.

Outdoor enclosures

Outside pens are often an excellent compromise for housebound cats, as they have the opportunity to experience all the sights and sounds without the risks.

Enclosures should ideally be attached to the home or if that isn't possible, conveniently located some distance from it. If the latter is your only option, you will need to transport your cat there in a secure basket and he won't be able to decide for himself whether it's a good time to go or not. The benefit of having the enclosure attached to your home is that at least one side of it (the wall of your property) is already constructed and if a cat flap is fitted your cat can choose when he goes into the pen.

The ideal construction is strong wire mesh on a wooden frame with a sloping roof of either more wire mesh or PVC corrugated sheeting (with a

UV filter) on a wooden frame. The latter offers all-year-round protection against the elements. The height of the structure should be at least 1.8 m (6 ft), to allow easy access for you and enable your cat to climb up high. Wooden platforms or shelving can be attached to the frame to enable the area to be used to its maximum potential.

Shelter should be provided inside the pen that's insulated and lined with a washable surface to make it easy to clean. Dry food can be left out for your cat in the shelter together with a warm bed. The pen should also contain a water bowl and sources of entertainment such as pots of grass or catmint, a wood pile and durable toys. A large, covered litter tray should also be included or, if the pen doesn't have a concrete base, an area can be dug over to offer a soil-based outdoor latrine.

Neighbours' cats can pose a problem, so the construction of any pen should make it as difficult as possible for other cats to gain access onto the roof or right up to the outside of the wire. Positioning pot plants outside the enclosure will provide your cat with that all-important camouflage.

WATERING YOUR CAT

• *Your cat's water bowl should ideally be ceramic or glass and large enough in diameter for him to drink from without his whiskers touching the sides.*

• *Fill the bowl to the brim so that your cat can lap without putting his head down, as cats like to keep an eye on things around them.*

• *Some cats prefer to drink from glasses, particularly those put by their owner's bed at night. If that's the case with yours, make sure there is a glass somewhere just for your cat.*

• *Running water is often attractive and electrically operated pet drinking fountains are now available.*

• *If your cat has access outdoors, providing a rainwater receptacle in the garden will be appealing to many cats as a good source of water.*

THE RIGHT RECEPTACLES

It's not always necessary to have a food bowl, particularly if you are feeding your cat a dry biscuit diet, but a suitable water bowl is a must in any situation.

If you feed your cat a wet-food diet or prefer a conventional feeding regime, you will have numerous food bowls to choose from. Ceramic or glass food bowls are probably the most sensible choice, as plastic receptacles scratch easily and can give off a slight odour that your cat may not like. Stainless steel is hygienic and easy to clean, but if your cat wears a collar, the constant clink of any disc or bell against the metal can be very off-putting for him. The bowl size or shape is down to your own personal taste, although many cats can be messy if eating from a flat plate and prefer to push food around a bowl that contains the food better. The only exception to the plate rule is in the case of the Persian or any breed with a flat face, which may prefer theirs as shallow as possible.

Your cat needs to drink plenty of water, particularly if he is on a dry diet. Most owners tend to offer water in a bowl beside their cat's food, but water can often be more attractive if it's located well away from routine feeding sites. The panel opposite offers some ideas for making water as attractive to your cat as possible.

TOILETING MATTERS

Litter trays are a necessary evil for cat owners – absolutely essential if your cat is housebound or has limited access outdoors and highly recommended even if your cat is free to roam.

Litter trays come in two basic styles:

- Open with a rim of varying depth but no cover
- Closed with a removable lid and, in some models, a cat-flap entrance

Within these two basic designs are size and shape variations, for example small and suitable for a kitten or triangular to fit in a corner. Many owners choose the covered type of tray, as they have the notion that these will offer some privacy while a cat uses its toilet with the added benefit that odour

Covered litter trays keep odour and soiled litter to a minimum but the single entrance/exit may be off-putting to cats in a multi-cat household.

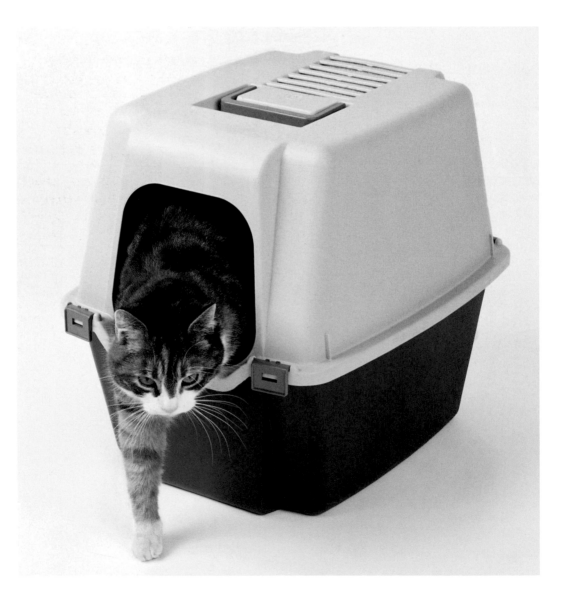

and visibility of soiled litter is kept to a minimum. While many cats adapt easily to a closed facility, there are some who feel vulnerable confined in a small space with only one available exit point, particularly if they share their home with other cats prone to using bullying tactics.

Self-cleaning litter trays are becoming increasingly popular, but once again these are marketed for the purchaser rather than the cat. They often make random movements or noises that can be disturbing for your cat and may even deter him from using it.

Polythene litter tray liners and litter deodorants are also available, but the overpowering floral odour and constant catching of claw in polythene can be unpleasant for your cat and may lead to soiling problems.

Litter is now manufactured in a wide variety of materials including paper, wood, silica, corn and fuller's earth. Many of these are lightweight, biodegradable and have excellent odour-neutralizing properties. Providing these litters are maintained properly and cleaned regularly they can be acceptable to your cat, particularly if you carry on using the particular material that he was weaned to as a kitten. The ideal substrate to meet your cat's preferences would probably be the fine sand-like litters because they best mimic the material that your cat instinctively favours – think African Wildcat! Research shows that most cats prefer a 3 cm (1¼ in) depth of litter in their tray.

The position of the litter tray is important. Choose a discreet corner, away from food and water, full-length windows and busy thoroughfares.

AND SO TO BED

Cats spend the majority of their time asleep, so it makes sense to focus on what provisions you are making for your cat's rest and relaxation. Unfortunately, it's not always easy to get it right.

Have you ever brought home a magnificent new cat bed only to have it firmly rejected by your feline companion in favour of the sofa or feather duvet upstairs? Why *do* cats think that the places their owners use are better than anything bought from a pet shop?

Cats favour warm places to sleep and many prefer them to have a strong familiar scent of their owners to give them a sense of safety and security. However, not all cats need the reassurance of their owner's smell when they are resting, so they may have several sleeping locations that rotate according to the position of the sun.

- *Make sure any cat bedding provided is washable, but don't clean it too frequently, as cats gravitate towards surfaces with a familiar scent so it's preferable to leave it unless it gets heavily soiled.*

- *Radiator hammocks are great for those heat-seeking cats, such as Siamese, Burmese and so on. They hook onto a radiator to enable your cat to gain the maximum benefit from the heat, but do remember to keep the radiator on a low setting!*

- *Cats love to sleep on their owner's lap, but if you really want to appeal to them, don't stroke them once they are settled – they want your warmth and smell, that's all!*

Cats spend most of their time asleep, and many will have several favoured sleeping locations based on where they feel warm and safe.

Opposite To encourage your cat to use a bed you've bought for him, place the bed in a raised position near a heat source. Do not clean the bedding too often as cats like a familiar scent.

If you can't resist purchasing a cat bed, or don't want to encourage your cat into the bedroom, then positioning it appropriately may be the key to its appeal. Place it in a raised position – many cats feel a little vulnerable sleeping on the floor – near a source of heat or an area in sunlight. If your cat likes his own space, then ensure that the bed is provided in a quiet area away from thoroughfares. Those with three high sides that surround your cat will keep draughts away and give him a sense of camouflage to avoid attracting attention – even a humble cardboard box will do the trick!

UP TO SCRATCH

Cats need to scratch to keep their claws sharp, mark their territory and exercise and stretch their muscles. Scratching posts come in all shapes and sizes and are an essential addition to your home.

If you fail to provide an acceptable area for your cat to scratch, then your carpets, furniture and wallpaper may get damaged. Once a cat finds an attractive area to scratch they will always return to it!

Scratching posts can be freestanding or designed to be fixed to a wall or floor. The freestanding type varies from short upright poles to floor-to-

ceiling modules with both vertical and horizontal surfaces made from a rough material such as sisal rope, corrugated cardboard or carpet. The panel type for wall fixing has similar surfaces for scratching and is useful if space is at a premium.

Any post or panel that is provided should be rigid, as cats prefer to scratch on a surface that provides resistance. Cats also have a height preference, so all scratching surfaces available should be tall enough to enable the cat to use it at full stretch. The location is also important. Scratching posts should be placed near a window or radiator in a room that your cat uses regularly, particularly if it is one of the larger designs that incorporates platforms and beds in the structure. Cats also like to stretch and scratch when they first wake up, so it's always beneficial to have an acceptable scratching area near your cat's bed. If your cat sleeps in your bedroom, provide a post there, as many cats love the base of a divan for an early morning scratch!

Cats need to scratch, particularly along with a stretch when they first wake up, and if you don't provide a suitable scratching post they will scratch your furniture, carpets and wallpaper.

Don't directly encourage your cat to show an interest in a new scratching post, as this could in fact put him off it. You can sprinkle a little dried catnip plant around the base to attract him.

STARTING FROM SCRATCH

When introducing a scratching post for the first time, don't encourage your cat to scratch or pay particular attention to the scratching post, as this may dissuade him from going anywhere near it! If your cat doesn't show any interest in the post, then sprinkle a little dry catnip plant over the base – this is an exciting herb for many cats – or some favourite cat biscuits. Playing a game with your cat with a fishing rod toy to encourage a connection between his claws and the rough surface will often succeed in promoting scratching.

IN-HOUSE ENTERTAINMENT

No matter how old or young your cat is, the benefits of play to his wellbeing are enormous, so make sure you invest in a few well-chosen toys to keep him on the go.

Cats will entertain themselves by chasing everything from a fly to a reflected beam of light on the wall, but it's still important to have some suitable toys to provide him with added encouragement and stimulation and which you can use to play with him to ensure quality time together.

There are two main types of toy: interactive toys (you play together) and solitary toys (your cat plays alone), and it's ideal to have a selection of both. The appeal of interactive ones is that they move, and since play is an expression of predatory behaviour, anything that can be chased and pounced upon will be thrilling.

There is no need to spend a fortune on expensive toys, as many ordinary household items, even rubbish, can be used to good effect. The

TOY FAVOURITES

Small fur-covered mice *Covered in rabbit fur that's sourced as a food by-product and the most 'natural' of cat toys.*

Hair bands *The covered elastic variety is just the right shape and size for retrieval games, if your cat is inclined to return it that is!*

Household rubbish *Screwed-up paper, foil, corks, walnuts, cardboard boxes and paper bags will all cost absolutely nothing, but will give your cat hours of entertainment.*

Fishing rod or wand toys *These can be agitated in front of your cat to get that predatory response. Anything with feathers on the end is popular, as is the string itself.*

Catnip toys *The best use large quantities of dried catmint flowers and leaves (rather than stalks), so check before you buy.*

guarantee to a lifetime's excitement is to maintain the novelty of all toys by keeping them hidden away, bringing them out in rotation. Anything that mimics the shape, size, movement or texture of a cat's natural prey is most likely to get even the couch potatoes of the feline world up and running.

Good games

Cats also enjoy playing games that explore other elements of their hunting behaviour apart from the stalk and pounce. The desire to explore and investigate new things is strong in cats and you can encourage this with a little ingenuity. If you can imagine the climbing, balancing, jumping, twisting and turning that a feral cat would execute in the course of a typical day, then you have some idea of what you need to reproduce at home.

Your cat probably likes to check out the contents of your bags when you return from a shopping expedition. This is part of an instinctive drive to seek out new sources of food rather than plain nosiness. If, once the contents are removed, those bags (or boxes) are placed on the floor with a sprinkle of catnip, a toy or a few biscuit treats inside, your cat will have hours of fun investigating how to retrieve the reward. Cardboard is also great to chew and particularly appealing to kittens. Always make sure that handles are removed from any bags to prevent your cat from getting his head caught. Novelty is also the key, so those items won't be exciting forever. Constantly changing them or moving them to different locations will keep your cat's interest.

Climbing games involve a little DIY, but are very popular with the more active cats. For example, if you attach a long panel of heavy-duty carpet to the wall, you have an instant cat climbing frame! Make sure that the wall is smooth before attaching the carpet panel using double-sided carpet tape. Secure the top and bottom with horizontal wooden batons attached through the carpet to the wall with screws. If this panel is situated near some shelving, it would give access to the top one and enable your cat to return to the ground via this route. Tall, modular scratching posts provide climbing opportunities, but the floor-to-ceiling models provide the best stability if they are anchored to the wall.

An example of an easy exploring game is placing a toy on a length of string under sheets of newspaper or a rug or mat on the floor. When you pull the string, the toy will move under the cover and be irresistible. There are many more ideas; you are only limited by your imagination!

Opposite Fishing rod toys are popular with cats. Agitate anything with feathers and string to elicit a predatory response.

Create a simple exploring game by placing a toy on a piece of string under a rug or sheets of newspaper. The movement of the toy under the paper will be irresistible.

Being cat-friendly

THE CAT'S ENTRANCE

A cat flap enables your cat to come and go through his own door. Modern examples come in a range of designs and sizes, and can also offer a variety of add-on features.

These include allowing you to adjust the access available, for example locking it at night or allowing entry-only usage after a certain time of day. Some are even large enough to accommodate dogs (and the more portly cats), and can now be fitted to non-standard doors and windows, such as double-glazed units.

In theory it sounds like a great idea; while you are out your cat is free to choose where he goes. Cats need to maintain a sense of control over their activity and this provides it. However, cat flaps can be a mixed blessing. When you are acting as doorman, your cat knows that he has to 'ask' you for entry and exit. This gives him a sense of increased security and the shut door represents a raised drawbridge, impervious to invasion. But a cat flap potentially allows invading cats to take advantage of the breach in defences and steal food. Any owner will recognize the way cats stare at a cat flap for ages before they leave or those that jump when the wind catches it. It sometimes isn't the perk we would like it to be.

To minimize the risk of other cats entering your home, it's possible to purchase flaps that offer the resident cat a degree of exclusivity of entry. A magnetic key that unlocks the flap can be attached to your cat's collar, but this relies on him not losing the collar and no other cat in the neighbourhood having a duplicate key! The process of disconnecting the locking mechanism also takes a few seconds, so hitting the flap at a run, with an adversary in hot pursuit, is like hitting a brick wall. Once your cat unlocks the flap and gets indoors, there is no guarantee that the other cat won't get in behind him. Modern versions work by reading the individual's microchip identification code under the skin on the back of the neck. While this system isn't perfect either, it resolves a few of the drawbacks. The bottom line is that a determined cat can probably break into any system.

Opposite Cat flaps offer both cats and owners some control and flexibility over available access, but be aware that they may make your cat feel vulnerable to invaders from outside.

ON THE MOVE

An essential piece of equipment for the cat owner is the cat carrier or basket – a secure container to confine your cat safely for trips away and journeys to the vet's surgery.

Under no circumstances consider allowing your cat to be loose in the car, no matter how placid his character. Accidents do happen, and should you need to brake hard or, worse still, be involved in a collision, your cat would be much safer in a carrier that has been secured with a seat belt.

The ideal carrier is strong and relatively lightweight – some can become extremely heavy once your cat is inside. It also needs to be secure – avoid the cardboard variety – and easily cleanable. Baskets with an opening at the top are preferable, as this enables you to lower your cat in from above, which is always an easier manoeuvre if you encounter any degree of reluctance from your feline. A lining of plastic sheeting, newspaper and then a towel or washable blanket will be sufficient to deal with any toilet mishaps en route.

It's now possible to get lightweight carriers that look like holdalls with fabric mesh at the front, which are easy to carry and can be folded and stored flat. Larger breeds can be accommodated by using one of the more substantial designs for dogs with wheels fitted, although quite how happy a cat would feel being dragged along on rough terrain is debatable!

COLLAR CORRECTNESS

For those cats with access outdoors there is often a need to fit a collar, either as a means of identification or to accommodate the magnetic 'key' for an exclusive-entry cat flap.

There are many types of collar made from a variety of materials; some even have a reflective surface for night-time use. The critical feature to look for in any of them is the ability to break under pressure and release your cat if he gets it caught on something outside. Many collars are fitted with an elastic section, but this is only effective if it's able to stretch enough for your cat to escape. Probably the ideal design is a collar with a breakable section that snaps when under sufficient strain – that is, your cat's bodyweight.

Loose collars can cause injury, so care should be taken when fitting your cat's collar for the first time. When you first fit it, your cat may tense his neck muscles, so always re-check the fit after a few minutes and adjust if necessary. A collar should be fitted surprisingly snugly; you should just be able to push two fingers through between the collar and your cat's neck. Once the collar is fitted snugly, it's best to cut off any excess of collar, leaving only 1-2 cm (½–¾ in) beyond the buckle.

Opposite Never allow your cat – no matter how placid – to travel loose in the car, but use a cat carrier or basket and always secure it with a seat belt.

Collars with a reflective surface are a good idea where visibility at night is desirable. Ensure that the collar is fitted properly, and that it has a breakable section in case it gets caught.

Understanding and tackling problem behaviour

Cats behaving badly?

There may be occasions when your cat exhibits behaviour that you find unacceptable but, before you presume that your cat is behaving badly, maybe you should explore other possibilities.

Living with cats should be a stress-free and completely enjoyable experience, but almost everyone at some stage will encounter a problem or become aware of a situation in their cat's life that is less than perfect. Any dilemmas or worries of this kind will hopefully be addressed in this section of the book. It also includes some guidance on the more serious issues that may occur, with practical suggestions on tackling the problem, or at the least finding someone who can help.

Cats are incredibly adaptable creatures, but sometimes a particular lifestyle or social situation will put them under pressure. Cats are ill-equipped to express their concerns openly – it doesn't pay in their world to be too honest about their emotions – and often internalize their stresses. This makes it a real challenge for you to establish that a problem exists, as your cat may appear perfectly normal. However, the clues are always there: he's sleeping upstairs under the bed when he used to sleep on the sofa; he's going out less and taking ages to leave the house; or he may just be sleeping more. Changes in your cat's pattern of behaviour and normal daily routines are the first sign of something being wrong, and if the issue remains unaddressed, he will reach a level of chronic stress that requires more demonstrative action. He will then behave in a way that looks, to the uneducated eye, dirty, bad, ill-tempered or downright inappropriate. To the perceptive cat owner this will be seen for what it is: a cry for help.

This is the time to seek advice and establish the root of the problem, as stress of this kind rarely goes away on its own. Problem behaviour often waxes and wanes and there is a temptation to presume each time that it's gone for good. If unacceptable or unexplained behaviour continues, on a daily basis or sporadically for a couple of months, take a deep breath and tackle it. Things at home or at work are often challenging enough, so accepting that the *cat* also has a problem can be hard to bear.

HOW TO GET HELP

Just devoting a few moments each day to monitoring your cat's daily routines could potentially prevent problem behaviour developing, by detecting changes at an early stage and seeking professional help.

The good news is that help is available and you never have to feel you are dealing with any problems alone. You should always seek veterinary

advice in the first instance when your cat exhibits unusual or inappropriate behaviour to rule out disease, illness or trauma. Only when a physical cause for the worrying behaviour has been ruled out will the vet consider an emotional or psychological origin. The case will then be referred to a veterinary behaviourist or professional pet behaviour counsellor to investigate further.

Intervention by a behaviour specialist will usually take place in your home, as a cat's environment greatly influences its behaviour and mood. Some professionals work from a clinic and use maps, video footage and questionnaires to get an impression of the environment to aid diagnosis of the problem.

If your cat starts exhibiting unusual or inappropriate behaviour, visit the vet first to rule out possible disease, illness or trauma.

While some behaviour specialists work from a clinic with the aid of questionnaires, film footage and maps, most prefer to observe the cat or cats in their home environment.

Once the causes and motivation for the behaviour have been identified, they will be explained to you and a programme put in place for you to follow under the guidance of the behaviour specialist. Cats don't respond that well to overt training, so work done to modify their behaviour differs greatly from that designed for a dog. The results are usually achieved by making subtle changes to your cat's environment or the way you respond to your cat. For example, litter trays may be provided in greater number or a cat flap may be removed from the door. You could be asked to ignore the inappropriate behaviour or initiate less contact with your cat to enable him to feel more in control of his social life. Occasionally, direct training can be used for specific individuals that may be particularly receptive. Behaviour or actions can be taught and performed on demand if they are positively reinforced or rewarded when they occur. Cats rarely if ever perform for praise alone, but those that are highly motivated by a certain food can be trained relatively easily. This may enable your cat to get used to doing something more acceptable when faced with whatever provoked the problem behaviour in the first place.

CHALLENGING CATS

There may be occasions when additional therapy is needed alongside the behaviour programme, particularly if your cat's problems have been evident for some time or whatever has prompted them can't be completely avoided.

Synthetic pheromones – chemical messages that are secreted from glands and work directly on the brain to influence behaviour – are frequently used in products that mimic naturally occurring feline facial pheromones, signalling familiarity and security. These can, if used correctly, reduce urine spraying by helping a cat feel more secure in its home. In intractable cases, some pharmaceuticals, nutritional supplements, homeopathy and herbal remedies may also be prescribed by the vet when necessary to give some extra assistance. Any treatment of this kind, whether or not it can be purchased without prescription, should always be authorized by a vet, as 'herbal' or 'natural' products are not automatically safe. Any administration of potent drugs should be monitored by the vet and dosage accurately calculated for the cat's bodyweight. You should follow any related instructions closely, as some drugs require a gradually reducing dose to be given at the end of a course rather than stopping abruptly. Blood tests may need to be taken to check your cat's liver function if drug therapy is used for prolonged periods.

Sometimes situations are so bad that the case in question represents nothing more than a square cat in a round house. No matter what you do, your cat will never fit in. Under these circumstances you may be counselled to consider re-homing your unhappy cat to an environment more suitable for his needs. These cats, when placed in sympathetic homes as singletons, blossom and rarely exhibit the problem behaviour again. However, the emphasis has to be on finding a new environment that is *significantly different* from the previous one and this requires frank disclosure of all the circumstances of the problem behaviour to any re-homing centre helping in the process.

MY CAT, MANGUS

It's a really difficult concept to embrace that problem behaviour can often be resolved by re-homing. Most owners believe that this constitutes 'giving up' and a form of abandonment. This really isn't the case as I have been involved in many situations where loving owners have bravely decided to do what's best for their cats and not for them. My own Mangus (a little Devon Rex) is a case in point. She lived previously with six other cats and she spent most of her time hiding under a bed to avoid relentless bullying and compulsively eating leather as a comforting way to get through the day. Within a few days of living with me as an only cat she blossomed into the happiest most demonstrative character you could ever wish to meet and leather goods hold no further attraction for her. Change the environment, remove the stress and the cat is transformed.

Prevention is always better than cure and many behavioural problems in cats can be avoided by making the right decisions and choices. See pages 178–203 for details of how to increase the likelihood of your household being a trouble-free cat-owning one.

IS YOUR CAT BEHAVING BADLY?

Identifying 'bad' behaviour is based on your subjective perception of what constitutes a problem, which may be vague as 'he's not himself' or observing that your cat's patterns of behaviour have suddenly changed.

More commonly, those issues brought to the attention of vets or behaviourists tend to be normal behaviour for the cat species but performed in an unacceptable or inappropriate situation. These would include cases of house soiling, urine spraying or other marking behaviour, inter-cat aggression, aggression towards humans, or damage caused by excessive scratching. In some instances, your expectations as owner may need to be reassessed, as they have to be realistic. Some problems that owners perceive as unacceptable, such as predatory behaviour and the frequent killing of rodents and birds, are normal for a cat and unrelated to any stress or negative experience. Attempting to prevent these from occurring could compromise

Aggression towards people may have been inadvertently reinforced when rough play as a kitten is unconsciously rewarded.

the wellbeing of your cat, so it may be necessary to adopt the philosophy of 'it's what cats do', no matter how unpleasant the behaviour appears to your human sensitivities.

Occasionally, owners inadvertently teach their cats 'bad' behaviour, resulting in some problems falling into the category of 'inappropriate learned behavioural responses'. These include aggression towards people represented in rough play, which you may have unconsciously rewarded and therefore reinforced in your cat as a young kitten, and attention-seeking behaviour – excessive vocalization or destructive habits – again which you may have unintentionally rewarded in an attempt to prevent damage or even by reasoning with your cat.

Some behaviours that are deemed unacceptable or inappropriate by owners are simply natural behaviours for the cat species – your expectations as owners my need to be reassessed.

Stress is a physiological response to life experiences, and a small amount is essential. As with humans, though, sustained unavoidable stress can be harmful.

There will always be a large number of cases of 'problem' behaviour that relate to illness or disease, as some physical ailments manifest themselves in abnormal behaviour. Some cases of house soiling can be related to bladder or bowel disease, and aggression can be caused by many different diseases or neurological problems. That's why it's always essential to consult a veterinary surgeon first before embarking on any self-help or behavioural advice, as the treatment and cure of any underlying physical problem will, with very few exceptions, resolve the problem behaviour. Behaviour that represents a medical warning sign is also looked at in detail in this section (see pages 154–155, 159–160, 163–165, 167–169 and 172–173).

IS YOUR CAT STRESSED?

Cats that display unacceptable or 'problem' behaviour are invariably suffering from chronic stress or anxiety. But being a territorial creature, it can be difficult to 'read' your cat in a stressful situation.

Stress is a physiological response to life experiences, both positive and negative, and it's actually essential in small quantities to prepare the body to deal with challenges. However, chronic unavoidable stress and the associated release of stress hormones in the body is harmful, leading to increased blood pressure, reduced gastrointestinal function and increased susceptibility to disease. Left unaddressed, it can also develop into a state of depression, a melancholy that overwhelms your cat and completely disrupts his ability to function.

Cats tend to develop strategies to cope with stress that can vary widely, depending on their personalities. For example, some individuals may spend less time eating, as they need to maintain increased vigilance at times of stress, whereas others will eat more as a form of displacement activity.

Factors that can potentially cause your cat stress may be found in his interaction with both people and his environment, but a significant proportion of the stress experienced by cats relates to their own species. If he is having to share resources with socially incompatible cats, it will be a constant nightmare for him, as is living in a neighbourhood overpopulated with cats.

Unfortunately, owners can inadvertently play a role in increasing their cats' stress levels. Some owners can be intrusive physically in the way they interact with their cats or generally inconsistent in the way they behave, leaving their cats uncertain of how to respond at any time.

The environment may well be the last thing you consider when assessing the welfare of your cat, as humans tend to perceive safety and love as being the most important provisions for their pets. However, being confined indoors or bored or having restricted access to hiding places or litter trays, for example, can be very stressful for your cat.

SIGNS OF STRESS

These include:

- *A reluctance to eat, groom, urinate and defecate or over-eating (depending on personality type)*

- *Increase in resting, feigned sleep and hiding*

- *Increased dependency or social withdrawal (depending on personality type)*

- *Defensive aggression towards other cats or people*

- *Extreme vigilance and a heightened response to sudden noise and or movement*

- *Lack of play activity*

- *Changes in patterns of behaviour, such as spending significantly more time indoors*

- *House soiling or urine spraying*

STRESS-RELIEVING STRATEGIES

If you can provide care for your cat that respects his needs both as a species and as an individual, you stand the best chance of preventing or reducing his experience of chronic stress. It's also worth remembering that experiences and situations that may stress your cat could be things you don't find worrying at all.

Marion and her tabby cat George were constant companions. He loved to be cuddled and they spent their days in perfect harmony. Sadly, George passed away and Marion couldn't face being alone so visited her local rescue cattery and found a tabby with a remarkable resemblance to George. She adopted George II but unfortunately he didn't like being picked up and cuddled and was quick to demonstrate the fact with tooth and claw. When I visited Marion I explained that not all cats, even if they look similar, like the same level of interaction with their owners. Marion wanted to persevere with George II, so she learnt to love him differently by allowing him to approach her when he felt like some attention rather than vice versa. Harry (renamed to aid the process), relaxed completely and had no further need to express his frustration through aggression.

The resources within the home, such as litter trays, feeding stations and beds, should always be provided in sufficient numbers to satisfy your resident cat or cats' needs. A good formula to use in order to calculate the appropriate quantity is one item per cat plus one extra, positioned in different locations. The number of cats kept in the home should be considered carefully, particularly if the local area already has a significant cat population as this can represent additional pressure.

Getting the relationship with your cat right is always a challenge, and being sympathetic to his particular emotional requirements as an individual is the key to him remaining stress-free. A confident, social cat will always want more attention than a timid one. If your cat has access outdoors, providing that access at regular times or at his request may avoid too many unwanted encounters with other cats outside. If your cat is kept exclusively indoors, a dynamic and challenging environment will entertain and exercise him, guarding him against boredom and frustration. Cats need to behave like cats for emotional and physical health, so providing your cat with a setting indoors that simulates a natural habitat, with objects to climb, for example, will give him the opportunity to play out his fantasies (see pages 112–117).

It's unrealistic to expect that all potential stress triggers can be removed from the lives of our domestic cats. If an owner or veterinary surgeon suspects that your

A reluctance to engage in previously popular play activities can be a sign of stress, as can increased dependency or social withdrawal.

cat is suffering from stress, there is no substitute for accurately establishing the specific source of stress and addressing it accordingly. If environmental and interactive changes are then made based on that assessment, for example an additional litter tray or an exclusive-entry cat flap, it can have a dramatic and positive impact on your cat's emotional and physical wellbeing.

The key to resolving these issues undoubtedly lies in a better understanding of the cat species and an accurate interpretation of the behaviour that gives an insight into the emotional state of the individual.

Cats need to behave like cats, so if your cat is kept exclusively indoors, provide a dynamic and challenging environment to entertain him and guard against boredom and frustration.

CAT VERSUS CAT

There are a number of reasons why aggression takes place between cats, either within the home or in territory outside, so it's important to consider the different triggers and understand why some degree of conflict is an inevitable consequence of your cat living in an environment surrounded by his own kind.

Although naturally territorial, domestic cats have become adept at inhabiting the same area by using scent marks, body language and vocalization to discourage unwanted close contact.

Cats are territorial creatures, which means they will actively defend their patch against the threat of invasion in order to protect the resources within it that they need to survive. Selective breeding for domestication over thousands of years has reduced this innate behaviour sufficiently to enable the modern pet cat to live whisker to whisker with unfamiliar cats. Those with access outdoors patrol their territory, leaving scent marks that enable large numbers to inhabit the same area without frequent confrontation and the risk of tooth-and-claw disputes. Most of your cat's communication, using scent, body language and vocalization, is about avoiding fights and increasing distance between individuals rather than encouraging contact.

Unfortunately, competition within a territory is not only about neighbour versus neighbour. Multiple cats within a single household can share space without having that important mutual bond. They often form cliques or splinter groups and cohabit without tears by agreeing to disagree and avoiding each other whenever possible. This doesn't mean that there won't be times when things have to be 'said' between members of separate factions to reaffirm who gets access to a particular resource at any specific time. This is when a cat may well employ passive bullying as a highly effective tactic of psychological rather than physical warfare.

Within any multi-cat group there will be potential bullies; all they need is a victim. A 'victim' is any cat that responds dramatically and with obvious apprehension to the posturing and threatening behaviour of another. The more the cat responds to this form of intimidation, the more the bully will 'up the game'. Some of the more determined types won't stop short of driving their victim from the home. These victims are the cats that develop stress-related illness as a result of the constant, unavoidable threat that the bully represents.

Common cat conflicts

Over and above defending their home range or at the very least the area they consider most significant to them against invasion, as most cats do, assertive cats in the neighbourhood may actively seek out opportunities to extend their territory and less-confident cats represent easy targets. If cats are unable to or are unsuccessful in the defence of their range, they could potentially become housebound, as their boundaries become pushed back so significantly that trips outdoors are deemed too dangerous. The cat flap or even an open door or window could potentially allow strange cats to invade the home and this can lead to aggressive behaviour from both parties. Surprisingly, there are occasions when the invading force meets no opposition from the resident cat, but this is largely down to fear rather than a positive acceptance of the encounter. Any such invasions can also cause friction between members of a multi-cat household, as it raises their anxiety levels and may potentially exacerbate rumbling tensions that have previously been maintained at a tolerable level. The sheer volume of cats in the neighbourhood can also have a similar effect, as their presence becomes a pressure that the cats within households are powerless to overcome.

In disputes between incompatible cats within a multi-cat household kept indoors, the same type of antagonistic interaction may take place and individuals become reluctant to venture out of one room except at very specific times as their territory becomes subdivided by the more confident cats. Active aggression (fighting) will occur if escape and avoidance opportunities are limited or absent. Some cats resort to fighting more readily than others depending on their genetics, sex and early experiences.

Any household with breeding females may also experience episodes of aggression, particularly when queens are protecting their kittens. These environments can be hotbeds of tension, often displayed passively, as there is frequently a mix of entire and neutered cats. Females coming in and out of season within the group can put further strain on relationships.

SIGNS OF BULLYING

These include:

- *Staring*

- *Claiming resting places or access to the owner by physically pushing another cat away*

- *Pouncing on a cat while asleep*

- *Blocking thoroughfares; sitting directly in front of the cat flap to deny entry/exit*

- *Blocking access to an indoor litter tray*

OTHER FLARE-UPS

An acute sense of threat from an external source can trigger cases of re-directed aggression from one cat to another if there are underlying tensions, and changes to existing cat groups can also ignite disputes.

Cats have a very keen survival instinct that utilizes an internal system referred to as the fight/flight mechanism, which releases adrenalin, pumping the muscles full of blood, to prepare the body for danger. This massive emotional response can be triggered by a sudden sound or movement, or the sight of another cat through a window, but the 'attack' may be accidentally launched towards an innocent cat if they happen to be in the wrong place at the wrong time. Relationships between two cats in a household can be irretrievably damaged under these circumstances.

It's perfectly normal for cats to resist the introduction of others to their colony, particularly if the newcomer is a mature adult. Any illness of a member can also trigger an aggressive episode, as it can disrupt their scent or cause behaviour changes, both of which could signal potential danger to other members. Some multi-cat households remain stable as a direct result of one member who singlehandedly maintains the group odour by interacting with all the other cats. Others remain outwardly stable if one cat dominates resources so successfully that a challenge is futile. If the pivotal cat in either situation should die, this can seriously disrupt the status quo and each cat has to establish new rights and potentially a new group.

There are a number of behavioural problems associated with inter-cat aggression. If the aggression displayed is largely passive, the first indication that there is conflict may be the development of inappropriate, abnormal or unacceptable behaviour. These include urine spraying, inappropriate urination and excessive scratching. Stress-related illness can also occur, as both the instigator and the recipient of the aggression can suffer from chronic stress as a result of the constant sense of threat; not all aggressive cats come from a place of confidence. Any persistent or recurrent viruses, feline idiopathic cystitis (FIC), conjunctivitis and inflammatory bowel disease (IBD) can all be triggered or exacerbated in such cases. FIC is a painful and distressing condition believed to have a significant stress component to its development and to the frequency and intensity of episodes. IBD is a relatively common condition, with symptoms increasing in severity at times of stress.

RUPERT TURNS NASTY

Poor Badger found himself in the wrong place at the wrong time. His companion, Rupert, had been staring out of the patio windows and seen Flossie from next-door in the garden. Immediately he became primed for a fight and stood with his gaze fixated on her every movement. In the meantime, Badger had fancied a bite to eat and was on his way to the kitchen. As he entered the room where Rupert was silently winding himself up into a frenzy, poor Badger came into sight and, in a split second, Rupert turned and attacked him with some ferocity. Badger escaped to the bedroom to reflect on the whole confusing event. All subsequent meetings between the two cats were tarnished by the memory of that episode for several weeks but now all is forgotten. Other cats are not so fortunate and if a gradual reintroduction doesn't work then owners may have to face permanent separation.

MAKING THE PEACE

Aggression between members of a multi-cat household can potentially be managed by seeking to identify the primary cause of the tension and attempting to deal with it or remove it.

If the trigger is tension between cats resulting from their incompatibility or constant competitive challenges, then you can adapt the environment to include additional resources that may limit the need for such relentless conflict. But bear in mind that these fellow residents may well have become irredeemably irreconcilable and re-homing one or more shouldn't be ruled out, as it could be the kindest option for all concerned. However, that doesn't stop you trying to establish peace.

Where tension exists between cats, adapting the environment may resolve the conflict. More frequent smaller meals may take the heat off feeding, for example.

Managing resources

All 'cat resources' – feeding areas, water bowls, litter trays, beds, toys, scratching posts, high perches and private places – should ideally be provided in the formula of one per cat plus one extra, positioned in different locations to ensure that all members perceive them to be in plentiful supply. If you have identified separate social splinter groups (see pages 84–86) and your space is limited within the home, then one per social group plus one extra may be enough. You can distribute dry food to a number of new permanent feeding 'stations' to give a sense of abundance and enable the cats to consciously decide an appropriate time to feed. Wet food can also be distributed in this way by providing frequent smaller meals to avoid competition at set mealtimes. Position the bowls so that each cat can eat without the need to turn its back on a potential adversary. Water is also an important resource to cats and several bowls placed in a variety of places throughout the home, away from the food, will potentially encourage the cats to visit more frequently.

Opposite Where practical, two separate points of entry and exit are a good idea as this avoids the risk of guarding or blocking by dominant cats.

Even if the cats have access outdoors, it's wise to provide indoor litter facilities, as it gives them the option to toilet in comparative safety indoors if there is any bullying going on outside in the territory. If it's practically possible, the provision of two separate entry and exit points to a property, such as cat flaps, doors or windows, avoids the risk of guarding or blocking, enabling even the most timid cat to get in or out unhindered.

Scratching posts should be located near entrances, beds and feeding stations to ensure that an appropriate surface is available in areas of potential competition, as cats will often scratch when others are around as a means of communicating territorial rights. Cats often prefer to observe activity from a high vantage point because this gives them a strong sense of safety, so provide plenty of opportunities for them to reach high places. Also consider the provision of private places, as every cat requires solitude and a safe place to rest, away from the risk of attack. Warm beds are also worthy of defence, so make sure that the appropriate number are available to avoid disputes.

If the inter-cat aggression has manifested itself in intense fighting between two individuals, the safest option is to separate them into different rooms for 24–48 hours until they have both calmed down. If a re-introduction at that stage still results in active fighting, it may be necessary to segregate them for a longer period and treat them like complete strangers meeting for the first time – see pages 191–193 on introducing a new cat to an existing one.

Returning from the vet

Episodes of aggression can occur at the most unlikely times when owners are often ill-prepared. One typical example is the reaction of the group to the return of a single member from a trip to the vet's surgery. Cats communicate predominantly using their sense of smell and the familiar

Opposite Cats with
excessively bullying
natures, most
commonly entire
males, are described
as despotic. Sadly,
they are often adept
at singling out the
old, infirm and timid
as victims.

communal odour that a group of cats creates helps to bond them. That scent changes when one cat takes a trip to the vet and acquires a mix of threatening and unpleasant smells from the surgery. This can cause a dramatic response when the cat is brought home and the others fail to recognize their companion. To avoid this happening to your feline family, keep the returning cat in a separate room for at least the first 12 hours (or overnight) to enable him to groom so that he re-establishes a familiar odour. You can assist this process by stroking and generally giving him affection, but be careful not to over-fuss a post-operative patient. Be guided by the vet or nurse, who will give you the appropriate aftercare advice.

ZORRO, THE DESPOT

Zorro was a Bengal with a soft spot for people but not cats. He was terrorizing the local cats on a daily basis and really pushed his luck one day when an elderly lady attempted to protect her cat in her own kitchen and was badly mauled as a result. Zorro's owner, Julia, was duly notified and action was demanded to keep him off the streets, so she kept him indoors for a week in the hope that he would become resigned to his confinement. Sadly this was not the case and he started to pace and spray urine constantly. It was eventually agreed that exclusive entry cat flaps would be fitted to each home, Zorro would be allowed out at specific times only (mainly at night) when other cats were safely indoors. It was difficult for many months and the problem was only resolved when Julia and Zorro moved to an area with very few house cats or cat flaps in sight and he was able to patrol and expand his territory at will without the need for constant conflict.

THE DESPOTIC CAT

Some territorial aggression exceeds what is considered by most to be acceptable. These cat bullies are often described as 'despotic', as they actively seek out territory defended by others to claim as their own.

These 'despots' will enter houses located over a wide area, attack the resident cats (and the owners if they get in the way) and spray mark vertical surfaces with urine before departing. The victims rarely fight back, as a 'despot' will choose them wisely and often pick relentlessly on the old, infirm or timid cats in the neighbourhood. Some pedigrees, such as the Burmese and more recently the Bengal, represent a surprisingly large percentage of the reported perpetrators. Entire tomcats (despots are usually male) are also likely to behave in a similar way, as will any domestic crossbreed that is particularly territorial.

Owners can become extremely distressed by these incidents, particularly as they occur within their own home, demanding that steps are taken by the owner of the bully in the view that the person in question is solely responsible for preventing future attacks. While it's entirely appropriate that these measures are put in place, the unpopular truth is that the victim's owner must also take reasonable steps to protect his or her property. The victim cats are clearly unable to deter intruders or defend their own territory, so the owners have to intervene in these cases.

There is some debate about whether or not these bullying cats are behaving abnormally for the species, but regrettably there is little evidence to suggest that their behaviour is anything but normal for the cat as a

territorial species. Domestic crossbreeds or 'moggies' have been selectively bred over many thousands of generations to moderate their territorial behaviour in order to live in built-up areas in close proximity to other cats. Expression of this behaviour is all a matter of degree, and cat owners all over the world should actually be grateful that this is not a more common problem!

Owners of despotic cats should confine them indoors at specific times to enable other owners in the area to allow their cats out then. Despotic cats should wear bells to warn of their whereabouts.

DEALING WITH A DESPOT

It's important to establish whether the cat is owned and neutered. If there is no evidence of an owner, it may be possible to request assistance for humane trapping, neutering and re-homing.

If you can locate the owner, it should be agreed that the despotic cat be confined indoors at night, if the fighting and property invasion occurs during the hours of darkness. The owner can feed the cat a late night treat to give some incentive to come in by a certain time. If the attacks occur during the day, the curfew hours should reflect that. All neighbours with victim cats should be informed that the aggressor is confined at specific times so that they know when their own cats are safe. The despotic cat should have a couple of bells attached to his collar in order that neighbours and their cats can hear him coming and take any necessary action if the curfew is broken.

The owner of the victim cat should block up their cat flap by locking it and placing a solid board over both aspects or close any doors or windows through which the aggressive cat entered the house. The aggressor's route into the garden should be established and blocked where possible. The victim cat should then be escorted into the garden by the owner if they show interest in going, but be sure to provide an indoor litter tray. If the victim wants free access outdoors in the future, an exclusive-entry cat flap should be installed (see page 119), but unfortunately no device will exclude the most determined cats from invading.

The aggressive cat's home should be adapted to ensure that he is provided with appropriate stimulation and resources, as enforced confinement could be stressful for him. Give him enough warm beds located around the house to allow him every opportunity to sleep and therefore fill

Provide plenty of warm beds around the house for despotic cats to sleep away their enforced confinement. Introduce active play sessions to use up excess energy.

the void of activity. Introduce active play sessions to use up energy, particularly early morning and evening or at other times when he is normally most active.

Some despotic cats are very determined to behave in this way and often the only way to resolve the heated disputes that arise between neighbours is to re-home them to areas with low cat populations.

INAPPROPRIATE TOILETING

Urine or faeces, or both, can be passed inappropriately when a cat soils the house. Inappropriate urination is one of the most common problems referred to pet behaviour counsellors.

Quantities of urine passed range from small spots to large volumes. Urine is normally voided on horizontal surfaces, but it may also be passed against vertical surfaces from a standing posture more normally associated with urine spray marking. The behavioural motivation for house soiling is usually due to a combination of factors and the cat will invariably be suffering from stress to some extent. The most common causes of inappropriate toileting indoors include:

Lack of early toilet training As a kitten, your cat may have failed to develop the habit of using a loose substance such as soil or proprietary litter materials. This results in him employing a degree of decision-making when he feels the urge to urinate or defecate and alternative sites being chosen that fulfil his particular criteria for a suitable toilet.

Removal of a favoured latrine site outdoors This site may well be outside the boundaries of your cat's own garden and any alterations, such as the introduction of a dog, another cat or removal of a particular flowerbed, may result in him looking to the comparative safety of indoors for a suitable alternative.

Bullying from cats outside Your cat may develop a general sense of insecurity outdoors if he has had any adverse encounters with other cats in the territory. Cats don't feel comfortable eliminating in the presence of such a danger, as they are particularly vulnerable to attack when doing so.

Tension within a multi-cat household An assertive cat within a household may use passive aggressive techniques, such as litter tray blocking, to intimidate another.

Aversion to the location of the litter tray Cats will be reluctant to use a tray if it's located in a site that renders it unattractive, such as too close to their feeding area, near an external full-length glass window, adjacent to the cat flap, in a busy thoroughfare, near noisy kitchen appliances or beside a door that is frequently used.

Aversion to the litter substrate Some cats can be particularly fastidious about the material used in their trays and certain materials, such as the wood pellets, silica granules or highly perfumed products, can be particularly unpleasant to cats. Polythene liners and deodorizing powders and fresheners can also be off-putting for some individuals.

Aversion to the litter tray Covered trays with flap entrances can seem like entrapment rather than privacy and this may deter timid cats from using one. It also traps the odours inside and creates an unpleasant environment if the tray isn't scrupulously cleaned. The trays used can also be too small for larger cats.

Unpleasant experience associated with the litter tray If a cat is scared or feels in danger while using the litter tray, it may deter future visits. Examples include an over-zealous owner attempting to medicate the cat while using the tray or a sudden loud noise or falling object.

Medical problem See pages 152–153.

Favourite sites
These tend to be the corners of rooms, particularly if they provide some camouflage like behind the television, or soft surfaces such as duvets or sofa cushions. Once a surface type or location is chosen, the cat will often return

The advent of house soiling is often related to your cat's usual latrine or litter tray becoming perceived as unsuitable. Soft furnishings or clothing are often favoured as alternative sites.

to it, drawn by the newly developed association between it and toileting. Some cats will also continue to use any provided litter trays or eliminate outdoors intermittently. Cats that feel particularly insecure will often choose items of their owners' clothing on the floor or places that smell strongly of them as latrines.

Keeping watch

If you are experiencing this problem with your cat, information gleaned about the nature of the urine passed and the frequency may help any vet or pet behaviour counsellor when making a diagnosis of the cause, so be vigilant. Urine with a pink tinge may indicate that there is blood present and very dark orangey-brown urine would suggest that it's highly concentrated. Pungent-smelling urine that has just been voided may indicate an infection. If excessively large quantities of urine are voided, it may suggest that your cat is retaining urine due to stress or discomfort. Normal urine should be pale yellow and not cloudy.

Should inappropriate toileting arise, keep a close watch to see the nature of the urine passed as it may be indicative of a health problem. Normal urine should not be cloudy.

TACKLING HOUSE SOILING

The first course of action must be to rule out any medical cause of inappropriate toileting. If nothing physical is wrong, it's likely that your cat is responding to a stressful situation.

Pain and discomfort can influence where cats prefer to eliminate and some cats develop negative associations with the litter facilities provided for them if they experience pain when using them. Urine and to a lesser extent faeces can be used to mark areas or objects of particular territorial significance and it's difficult to establish, without professional help, whether the problem is related to emptying the bowel and bladder or making some form of marking gesture.

Failure to accurately identify the primary motivation for the behaviour doesn't necessarily prevent you from taking certain action that will do no harm and probably enhance your cat's feelings of security and reduce stress. Even if your cat has unlimited access outdoors, this is the time to introduce attractive, safe litter facilities in the home. How attractive a particular tray will be is largely dependent on the idiosyncrasies of your individual cat, but there is a popular format that appeals to the majority.

Removing the evidence

First, soiled areas should be cleaned as thoroughly as possible to remove any residual odour that may be luring your cat back and encouraging a habit to develop. Cleaning is a challenge in itself, as some surfaces such as furniture and carpets soak up the urine and draw it into the layers beneath where it degrades and produces the telltale stench associated with a long-term soiling problem. If carpet is affected, it should ideally be removed and destroyed, together with any underlay. The floor beneath the soiled area should be treated with an appropriate product, preferably recommended by your vet or a pet behaviourist, before any new carpet is introduced.

Once the soiled areas have been thoroughly cleaned, it's useful to alter the site enough to make access difficult. Affected rooms can be closed, but if the soiling has occurred in a room that is used frequently or can't be shut off, moving furniture or placing an upturned box over the area may be sufficient. Deterrents, such as pepper, citrus peel or commercially available products, should be avoided, as they can sometimes increase your cat's stress levels and merely redirect him to soil in a new area, thereby extending the damage.

Reassessing trays and litter

The number of litter trays introduced should reflect the size of any multi-cat group (see the formula on page 132) and be located in different areas rather than concentrated in one convenient spot. This prevents any opportunistic cats from blocking access to the more timid individuals. The trays should ideally be located in corners so that the cat has the protection of walls or furniture on two sides to avoid ambushes from behind. You can provide covered trays, but don't presume that these will automatically be favoured over the more exposed open ones. In fact, covered trays offer the perfect opportunity for further intimidation and bullying, as cats can be trapped inside or tackled from above when the resident bully works out that he can sit on top of the tray when his adversary uses it.

The size of the tray should be large enough to enable your cat to comfortably move round in it and choose his spot carefully. If your cat has a tendency to rise as he urinates and deposit urine in a semi-spraying stance, it's useful to acquire high-sided trays so that the jet can be contained within it. The litter material should be a fine sand-like consistency without added 'fresh' odours or crystals designed to control smells. Purchasing a clumping variety will enable the tray to be cleaned daily without urine-soiled litter accumulating, as it dries to a hard lump that can easily be removed. The depth of the tray should enable digging and most cats favour a depth of at least 3 cm (1¼ in). If the tray is completely emptied once a week and washed with hot water and a mild detergent before refilling, it should remain untainted but encourage continued use. Litter tray liners and powder deodorants should be avoided as yet another obstacle to successful and stress-free toileting.

RAISE THE DRAWBRIDGE

Pip started spraying in the kitchen, shortly after his owners installed a cat flap, when the neighbour's cat came in through the new entrance to eat his food. Pip's owner, Jonathan, worked from home and had fitted the flap to provide his cat with the freedom to come and go when he was busy. After careful deliberation Jonathan decided to abandon the cat flap for the time being and he attached solid boards to the front and back of the door to give the appearance once again of an impenetrable structure. The sprayed areas in the kitchen were cleaned thoroughly and Pip was entertained with games, toys and frequent small meals. Jonathan gave access to his study during the day for Pip to visit him and resolved the back door issue by allowing Pip to come and go through the study window. Pip returned to his normal relaxed self once the new regime was established.

URINE SPRAYING

Urine spraying is a form of territorial marking behaviour that usually involves the cat depositing small amounts of urine on a vertical surface, although horizontal surfaces may be targeted by squatting.

The cat will back up towards a vertical surface in a standing position and lift its tail upright. A small jet of urine will be deposited while the cat treads with its back paws and the tip of its tail twitches or shivers. Cats may even deposit a small urine marker on horizontal surfaces by squatting. Research has shown that cats can distinguish between urine deposited vertically and horizontally, so it's possible that secretions from the anal glands are involved when the cat sprays, and the urine certainly appears more viscous and oily than normal. Locations chosen for spraying tend to be in full view in areas of particular territorial importance where the cat feels challenged.

All cats – male, female, neutered and entire – are capable of spraying urine in the right circumstances. In sexually active males and females, the urine mark

represents an invitation that communicates their readiness for mating. In neutered cats it has the opposite purpose, as it deposits a scent that enables territory to be utilized by a number of cats without coming into direct contact with each other. The freshness or otherwise of the scent will indicate when the other cat deposited it and therefore whether it's safe or not to enter the area.

There should be no need for your cat to spray urine indoors in a domestic setting, since this should represent a safe haven for the resident, or residents. If there is tension between the members of a multi-cat group or a single cat feels threatened, they may resort to employing urine spraying to address the conflict. The spray marks are focused on areas where the cat feels particularly vulnerable. Spraying can also be used as an attention-seeking tool or in situations when a cat is frustrated. Passive aggression can also be associated with urine spraying under certain circumstances. So, it's easy to see that this behaviour is a complicated and even multi-purpose communication device for your cat!

Urine sprayed vertically is a form of territorial marking behaviour, and research has shown that cats can distinguish between urine deposited vertically and horizontally.

TACKLING URINE SPRAYING

It's important to identify the area where the spraying took place, as the location may well give you a good indication of the original stress trigger, which can then be addressed.

If, for example, the urine spray marks were deposited adjacent to a cat flap or external door or window, it's likely that the problem lies outside the house. But if internal walls or doorways were originally anointed, it's a strong indication that the enemy is *within* the home and some tension exists between some members of a multi-cat household. Identifying the cat responsible is also important, as not all sprayed urine is deposited in sight of the owner. Insecure cats with non-specific pressures may spray urine in response to environmental changes such as new furniture, building work or decoration, particularly if they are kept exclusively indoors, although this is rarely a primary cause. There is usually another cat behind the problem somewhere and the challenge is to identify him and then reduce the threat he represents.

Security measures

While identifying and dealing with the trigger is essential for a complete resolution of the problem, measures can be taken that will potentially increase the cat's sense of security and decrease the need to spray urine. If you think the stress factor is coming from outdoors, after assessing the pattern and location of spraying, remove any full-length curtains, or pin them up temporarily, that are being anointed. Full-length glass windows or doors can give strange cats the opportunity to get far too close to the home, so block lower glass panels by using opaque film to increase your cat's camouflage in the home. Provide high vantage points near windows to enable your cat to view potential danger from a secure position.

Clean the sprayed sites with a 10 per cent biological washing powder solution using warm water. Rinse immediately afterwards and then spray with a light mist of surgical spirit to break down the compounds that produce the odour that's encouraging your cat to return to the site to 'top up' his scent. Alternatively, your veterinary surgeon may recommend a commercially manufactured product that is effective at removing the odour.

Provide safe, attractive indoor litter facilities in the formula of one tray per cat in the household plus one extra, located in different areas in the home. Place new feeding bowls at sites where your cat has sprayed to provide a more positive association with the location. If the problem has been identified as friction within a multi-cat group, ensure that all the cat resources, such as beds, scratching posts, litter trays and hiding places, are provided in sufficient number to satisfy the needs of all the cats and reduce competition. If possible, install a second entry and exit point to the home to avoid any cat being denied the ability to enter or leave. If the cat flap itself is the cause of the insecurity and a strange cat has come in, it may be useful

to temporarily block the cat flap, by covering it completely on both aspects to appear like a solid door, and allow your cat to come in and out through a door or window on demand.

Synthetic feline facial pheromones (see page 127), available in spray form or in a device that plugs into an electrical socket and emits the pheromones, can potentially reassure your cat and make him feel more secure. These products may be useful as part of the overall changes you are making, so speak to your veterinary surgeon and he or she will advise accordingly.

Feelings of insecurity can cause your cat to start spraying so provide high vantage points near windows so he can view potential danger from a position of safety.

Refocusing your cat's mind

Breaking the cycle of anxious behaviour associated with urine spraying can be difficult. Cats often pace from window to window repeatedly and vocalize prior to spraying, indicating a degree of ritual and therefore tough to stop. Introducing a scheduled and exciting play session at those specific times when your cat has been preoccupied with spraying may focus his mind on more positive activity. Cats have very specific likes and dislikes when it comes to toys, so choose carefully to ensure that you capture your cat's complete interest. Playing in frequent short bursts is more attractive to him than a prolonged marathon. Using a fishing rod or wand toy to stimulate the movement of prey may be sufficiently exciting to distract your cat, giving you the opportunity to lure him away from the area where the pacing is most prevalent.

MEDICAL WARNING SIGNS – HOUSE SOILING AND URINE SPRAYING

There are a number of medical reasons why a cat may urinate inappropriately or spray urine, particularly if the sprayed quantities are large, as this is not normally associated with marking behaviour.

The most common cause of urine soiling is cystitis or bladder problems referred to as feline lower urinary tract disease (FLUTD). Bladder stones can cause blood in the urine, difficulty in urinating or pain when passing urine, as can a condition called feline idiopathic cystitis (FIC), which is relatively common and considered to be stress related. Susceptible individuals at risk of developing FIC are overweight neutered cats living indoors or with limited access outdoors in multi-cat households.

Problems such as bladder tumours or abnormalities in the urinary tract also need to be ruled out in cases of house soiling. Renal failure or loss of function of the kidneys can cause excessive drinking and urination, and this can be enough to result in inappropriate urination because cats suffering these conditions use their trays more excessively than normal and pass larger volumes of urine. Diabetes also has similar symptoms and therefore may cause the same behaviour.

Pain or mobility problems, such as those associated with arthritis, can also make the use of cat flaps or awkwardly located litter trays difficult and the adoption of an area where toileting can occur more easily is a potential consequence.

Diseases such as feline immunodeficiency virus (FIV) and feline leukaemia virus (FeLV) may also cause symptoms that lead to house soiling. Any disease causing urinary incontinence will lead to urine being passed as a cat rests or sleeps.

Urine spraying may be associated with urinary tract disease and has even been known to occur in cats with impacted or infected anal glands.

DID YOU KNOW...?

- *Studies have shown that cats may be more likely to exhibit signs of lower urinary tract disease (cystitis) during periods of inclement weather when they spend more time exclusively indoors.*

- *Cat urine glows under ultraviolet light making it easier to spot areas of carpet requiring treatment if your cat has soiled in the house. Hand held lamps can be purchased specifically for the purpose of detecting urine stains.*

Urinary incontinence causes urine to be passed while your cat is asleep. Since cat urine glows under UV light, special lamps make it easier to find the soiled spots.

Inappropriate defecation may occur if the cat is suffering from disease of the gastrointestinal tract, which causes diarrhoea, colitis or constipation. Any medical condition that causes an increased volume or frequency of defecation, decreased control or faecal incontinence or pain when defecating could be implicated.

CAT VERSUS OWNER

There are many motivations for your cat displaying aggression. It's an intrinsic part of a cat's survival strategy and almost inevitable that pet cats will show some aggression at one stage or another.

There are some common causes of aggression, but taking on the diagnosis of what's motivating your cat's aggressive behaviour yourself can be a dangerous move, as an incorrect assessment may lead to an escalation of the problem if tackled inappropriately. A penetrating bite wound from a cat usually doesn't bleed profusely, as the canine teeth create a puncture hole that quickly heals over. However, all the bacteria from the cat's mouth are then trapped in the tissue under the skin and infection is highly likely, so do seek medical attention as soon as possible.

Lost lessons

Kittens fight each other when they are young and engage in enthusiastic rough and tumble fights that are interrupted if they become a little too violent and one of them runs away or bites back particularly hard. This enables the kittens to learn to inhibit their biting when playing. Unfortunately, when humans attempt the

Young kittens engage in rough-and-tumble games, which will be abandoned if one becomes too violent. This teaches them not to be too rough with one another.

same kind of games, using their hands, they often reinforce the highly excitable behaviour and encourage a kitten to grow up biting and scratching in the name of play with an intensity that can cause injury. Your cat's preferred target of hands will soon extend to include bare feet and when adult he will ambush you by pouncing on both feet and hands at every opportunity.

Another important lesson that a cat should learn as a youngster is the ability to deal with frustrating situations. So if your cat missed out on discovering that frustration is an inevitable part of life, he may turn to

Humans can inadvertently encourage and reinforce excitable but inappropriate behaviours in the name of play such as scratching and biting hands.

aggression to express his rage when things don't go his way. Reactive individuals may attack owners as a release for the 'emotional upset' of late dinners, locked cat flaps or any other slight annoyance. There is some evidence to suggest that frustration is learned during the weaning process and that hand-rearing often fails to mimic this and therefore may produce adults that are easily annoyed.

Aggression can be used both offensively and defensively, and when fear-based it's purely a survival strategy in circumstances when the cat feels vulnerable and in danger. Many cats deprived of early socialization with humans will remain fearful in their presence, and unwanted advances and attention can result in the use of aggression as a deterrent. If the threat of aggression doesn't result in the person or persons withdrawing, unfortunately teeth and claws will then be employed to enable the cat to escape.

Other causes

Other types of aggression can inadvertently be taught to cats. Some cats that are confident and assertive can become, given the right circumstances, controlling and manipulative using aggression and threat to dictate their owners' movements and actions in the home. These cats often spend the majority of their time indoors with owners that historically have been compliant to their cats' every demand.

There are occasions when it's possible for humans to become the victims of re-directed aggression in response to movement or touch (see page 136 for the outcome of being in the wrong place at the wrong time). Owners often reassure their cats when they see them alarmed by the sight of another outside and pay the price as they become the victim of an intense attack. This emotional response can be so new and unusual to your cat that all future contact with you could trigger a similar state of mind. This is further compounded by your obvious sense of apprehension in anticipating attack, and it doesn't take long for all trust to drain out of the relationship. Aggression can also be motivated by pain and disease – see pages 159–160.

Some aggression has a cause that's not quite so easy to identify. These are dangerous cases since, should the trigger fail to be identified, the cats will potentially show 'unprovoked' aggression at any time. If a pattern can't be established or the aggression is accompanied by bizarre behaviour before or

Aggression that has a trigger that is not easy to identify can be dangerous. If there is strange behaviour before and/or after an attack, there may be a physical cause so consult your vet.

after an attack, it's possible that it has a physical rather than a behavioural cause (see pages 159–160). These are not situations to tackle alone; cats exhibiting aggression of unknown origin, known as idiopathic aggression, can be extremely dangerous and measures should be taken quickly to ensure everyone's safety. A veterinary examination is essential.

RESOLVING HIS AGGRESSION

Play aggression is easily prevented by ensuring that human body parts never form part of a game with your pet cat. There are numerous toys available that are attached to rods or sticks to enable easy manipulation so that your hands can remain associated in your cat's mind with gentle stroking, holding and feeding rather than predatory play. However, cats that exhibit assertive aggression have to be handled with care.

Aggressive posturing only works if the victim is taking any notice, so treating this with a period of healthy neglect together with protection from stout footwear and clothing usually does the trick. If this strong signal of 'non-reward' is consistent and you offer your cat opportunities to indulge in more natural, acceptable pastimes, it's possible that the problem may resolve without further intervention.

The best resolution for fear aggression requires patience in gradually exposing your cat to the source of that fear so that he learns that people are not as dangerous as he thought. Fearful cats are at their happiest when they are cohabiting with you rather than forming one half of a relationship. If you ignore a fearful cat by not offering him eye contact, verbal communication or direct approaches, he will feel less threatened and therefore be less likely to show aggression. But if the cat in question is injured or needs to be handled for its own safety, you would need to take precautions against a potential attack.

Time usually heals cases of re-directed aggression, but owners need to refrain from touching their cats when they are fighting imaginary battles. Even when your cat bursts through the cat flap after an altercation outside, you may risk an aggressive episode, so if the signs are there, stay away until your cat has calmed down. Most cases of aggression need assistance from a professional pet behaviour counsellor, but in the first instance safety is paramount. If you are the victim of an

THE GINGER NINJA

Tigger was a six-month-old ginger kitten with attitude. His owner, Karen, asked me to visit as she could no longer handle the unruly youngster. He would rush at her, biting her hands and feet at every opportunity. It is rare for young cats to show aggression in this way so I was suspicious that the clue to this behaviour was in Tigger's upbringing. Sure enough, Karen's partner, Tim, had been keen to involve himself in Tigger's care and spent many hours rolling him around on the carpet while the little ginger kitten chewed enthusiastically on Tim's fingers. Undoubtedly a great game but Tigger had learnt that hands and feet were appropriate targets for play and that biting hard was allowed. In every other way Tigger was the perfect kitten, so a little training with fishing rod toys and avoidance of any opportunity to see moving fingers and toes soon got him on the road to forgetting this unfortunate habit.

aggressive attack, seek medical attention for bites and severe scratches and arrange for a veterinary examination to rule out any medical cause. In the meantime, avoid contact with your cat (don't approach, make eye contact or communicate verbally), protect your legs and arms with thick clothing and shut him out of the bedroom at night.

Cats showing assertive aggression must be handled with care. Never use body parts as part of a game, but choose toys attached to rods or sticks instead.

MEDICAL WARNING SIGNS – BEING AGGRESSIVE

Chronic pain or even the association of pain with handling may cause your cat to behave defensively, leading to fear-related aggression. This will always be preceded by body language strongly advising you to withdraw.

This behaviour may also be directed at other cats in response to an underlying sense of vulnerability due to illness. Changes in the scent profile of a sick cat could potentially influence the behaviour of other members of a multi-cat group, so under these circumstances you should arrange a veterinary examination for both the aggressor *and* the victim. Diseases and conditions associated with pain include arthritis, feline lower urinary tract disease (FLUTD) and any trauma such as injuries from traffic accidents or cat bites. Any cat suffering from these conditions may display aggression to deter unwanted handling.

Other diseases such as feline immunodeficiency virus (FIV), feline infectious peritonitis (FIP), toxoplasmosis and encephalitis have also been associated with aggression. A common condition of the elderly cat is an overactive thyroid gland, called hyperthyroidism, causing weight loss, increased appetite and often a general increase in aggressive or short-tempered behaviour.

The aggression shown is usually defensive in nature, in response to approaches or some form of physical contact. Occasionally, aggression can be displayed that appears, at first sight, to be unprovoked and extremely intense in nature. It may be preceded by unusual behaviour and after the aggressive outburst your cat may appear confused or distressed. This may be an indication of seizure activity or brain disease, so in these cases seek veterinary intervention as a matter of urgency. In the meantime you should take precautions to protect yourself until the problem is addressed, as these attacks can occur without warning.

If your cat has never shown aggression before and suddenly attacks another cat or you, it's a significant indicator that he may be ill or in pain. Be sure to get veterinary advice immediately, as you may need to be given practical guidance about handling your cat prior to veterinary examination and any necessary treatment.

THE NERVOUS CAT

Adult cats are usually confident enough to face what life throws at them, but if they aren't exposed to the full range of domestic happenings early on, they could flee from the most innocuous events.

As discussed throughout this book, your cat's behaviour and character are shaped by a complex mix of influences relating to the species, his individual genetic make-up and his experiences as a kitten. These elements create your cat's unique personality, for instance bold, confident, reactive and sociable. Cats' highly developed survival instinct enables them to assess danger quickly and act accordingly. The response to that perceived danger is often to escape rather than stand and fight.

Some cats are also born with a predisposition to anxious behaviour, and even with the opportunity to socialize at the appropriate age they fail to learn that domestic life is comparatively free from danger. This state of anxiety means that the cat experiences an emotion, particularly in unfamiliar situations, that is an apprehensive anticipation of something bad happening. This may increase to fear if a specific stimulus is confirmed, via the cat's own

A convenient hiding place, such as under a bed or chair, provides an escape from danger and a safe haven for a nervous cat.

mental assessment, to be dangerous. Fear is the innate trigger for the release of adrenalin that prepares the body for tackling life-threatening situations by fighting, escaping, freezing (in the hope of remaining undetected) or attempting to appease the dangerous adversary, with cats tending to favour the second option in any event, as already explained.

These nervous cats are easy to spot by their patterns of behaviour. For example, they will startle easily, run and hide at the sound of a doorbell and even flinch when you reach out to or walk past them. Nervous cats always retreat rather than face life's challenges so spending lengthy periods under beds or hiding in the wardrobe will be the timid cat's location of choice should anything occur that is out of the ordinary. Many people presume that cats behaving in this way must have been cruelly treated in the past, although this is not necessarily the case. Persistent timidity of this kind predisposes nervous cats to developing conditions such as feline idiopathic cystitis (FIC) and potentially any other disease or illness with a stress component.

Positive thinking

Owners often behave in a certain way around nervous cats, presuming that hushed voices and movement from room to room on the tips of their toes is the right strategy to adopt to avoid scaring them. Unfortunately, the air of tension in the home that this creates merely fuels the cat's anxiety. Acting normally and feeling relaxed as a consequence would have a more positive impact. Constant attempts to communicate and demonstrate your love, involving seeking out your nervous cat and extracting him from a hiding place or focusing on him as he enters a room, are also undesirable for a timid cat, often resulting in making you look threatening and obtrusive. It's better to give a nervous cat a 'cloak of invisibility' to allow him to move around the home without feeling that he is the focus of attention. This sense of relaxed cohabitation involves no direct eye contact, verbal or physical communication unless your cat directly initiates it by his own behaviour (see pages 94–95).

Food treats can be used to create positive associations and develop a bond between you and your nervous feline. Offering small amounts of meat, fish or other tasty treats in a bowl is useful in encouraging him to explore various rooms in the home or spend time in close proximity to you. Try offering the same treats on the palm of your outstretched hand placed on the floor to entice your cat to take food directly from you.

Positive play interaction could also reap rewards, as many cats find games irresistible. Using a toy, attached to a string and a long rod, will enable your cat to enjoy the game fully without feeling that you are too close.

Constant reassurance of timid behaviour in response to non-threatening events will merely reinforce the nervousness of your cat, so it's best to ignore it and give positive rewards – whatever may motivate your particular cat – for calm behaviour.

Finally, it's important to understand a nervous cat's expectations of life. Hiding under a bed may seem like a wretched existence, but if this is perceived by your cat to be an escape from danger and a safe haven, his emotion will be one of relief rather than any directly negative feeling.

MEDICAL WARNING SIGNS – BEHAVING DIFFERENTLY

There will be occasions when you may observe changes in your cat's behaviour that are subtle and that don't involve the more obvious displays of aggression or house soiling.

Such a change may simply be a case of your previously confident cat suddenly appearing nervous and 'edgy'. Single, profoundly frightening incidents can sometimes be enough to create a persistent state of anxiety, but it could also be a sign that your cat is unwell. Most vets understand how important it is to listen to owners who say, 'he's just not himself.'

In addition to what they glean through examination, vets rely heavily on information given by the owners, which makes your observations of changing patterns of behaviour very important.

Owners need to be tuned into their cats and have a degree of understanding of their routines and habits, and how the seasons, weather and other factors influence their normal activities. If your cat shows an obvious change in those routines, such as spending more time indoors than is usual for the season, sleeping under the bed, avoiding a particular room or showing fear in a familiar, non-threatening situation, this may be an indication that he's responding to an internal problem and experiencing pain or discomfort, or feeling ill in general.

A cat's natural response to trauma or illness is to find a quiet and safe place, away from predators, to rest and heal damage or fight infection and disease. Therefore, any cat that returns home and immediately seeks out a dark cupboard where it remains for a significant period of time is probably ill or injured. More discreet changes can take place as cats stop performing certain behaviour that has started to become painful or difficult due to mobility problems. Many cats with arthritic changes in their joints will stop scaling fences in the garden and jumping up onto high surfaces. They may also adopt a bunny-hopping gait when coming downstairs or an unkempt coat due to loss of the flexibility needed for grooming. All of these shifts in behaviour are a possible indication of arthritis and worthy of investigation by a vet.

One of the many challenges facing veterinary medicine is the inability to communicate directly with the patient regarding its symptoms, so vets rely heavily on information gleaned from the owner, in combination with physical examination and diagnostic tests. Accurate diagnosis can be greatly assisted by your vigilance and observation of changing patterns in the behaviour of your cat.

THE OVER-GROOMING CAT

Your cat can focus excessive grooming on any area easily accessible to his tongue, but the most common sites are the abdomen, flanks and inside the thighs and forelegs.

Most cases of over-grooming are prompted by a skin problem or pain. If medical conditions are investigated and ruled out, the problem may be stress-related.

A skin problem, such as a flea allergy, can prompt over-grooming in cats. Broken hair shafts, bald patches and trauma to the skin can all be caused by over-grooming.

Stress in cats, rather like with us, works in layers and a combination of potential stress-inducing factors can have an impact on your cat's emotional state. Cats have very limited ways of expressing their emotions, particularly if they are naturally ill-equipped to cope under pressure. The easiest option for some is to develop a coping strategy involving one of the few normal activities readily available, such as sleeping, eating or grooming. It's no coincidence that cats frequently sleep for excessive periods, over-eat and over-groom.

As bald areas are created through over-grooming, your cat will often extend the area to the nearest patch of hair until significant proportions of his coat have been damaged or removed. The damage can be caused by your cat licking, chewing and plucking in order to remove debris during normal grooming and maintenance sequences but to excessive levels.

Over-grooming can be a form of self-appeasement or displacement activity in response to an environmental stress factor and therefore a 'normal' strategy under those circumstances. Unfortunately, it can be taken to a level that causes your cat to suffer broken hair shafts, bald patches and trauma to the skin. He may also experience vomiting or gastrointestinal problems as a result of the large volumes of fur that he is swallowing in the process.

Cats that over-groom for purely psychological reasons are comparatively rare. When this occurs, it's often a Siamese or similarly sensitive and reactive Oriental breed that is affected and they usually mostly use a plucking action to remove their fur in clumps. The reason for the problem is frequently found to be their response to a lifestyle pressure such as lack of stimulation, an over-attachment to their owner or tension with other cats in the household.

However, most cases of over-grooming in cats are prompted by a skin problem or pain. Chronic stress can affect an individual cat's immune response and the constant release of stress hormones can cause the skin to become particularly sensitive, resulting in primary dermatological disease or the worsening of an existing skin problem.

COPING WITH OVER-GROOMING

Once medical conditions have been investigated and ruled out, over-grooming can be presumed to be primarily stress-related, but it's probably wise, given the strong implication of skin problems, that flea control is vigorously maintained.

It's essential that you seek advice from your vet on flea control treatment for your cat, to be given at the appropriate intervals. Modern veterinary formulations don't rely on the flea biting the cat to ingest the substance that kills it. A drop of liquid is applied to the skin on the back of your cat's neck and is absorbed into the hair follicles. The flea dies on contact with the hair before it bites, so this formulation is particularly useful if your cat has a sensitive skin.

Medical warning signs

If your affected cat is suffering the underlying effects of a skin problem or pain (as is the case with most cats displaying over-grooming), he will lick, chew, pluck or bite areas of fur and skin, causing alopecia (hair loss), trauma to the underlying skin and, in extreme instances, damage to the tail requiring partial or complete amputation. Diseases associated with over-grooming and self-mutilation include feline idiopathic cystitis (FIC). Over-grooming associated with bladder disease occurs in response to the localized pain and usually focuses on the lower abdomen, bottom and inside of the thighs. Another recently identified condition called feline hyperaesthesia syndrome may also be significant, as affected cats exhibit exaggerated responses to touch and suffer intense episodes of twitching and rippling skin, accompanied by tail chasing and biting.

The most common cause of over-grooming in cats is the itch that occurs with flea allergic dermatitis. Cats develop an allergy to flea saliva, and when a flea bites their skin, it irritates them and causes intense itching. This in turn encourages the cat to groom in response and an itch–scratch cycle is created that continues often until veterinary intervention takes place and the underlying irritation is addressed.

Cats can also develop sensitivities to certain foods, pollens, trees and plants and even house dust mites – all of which can result in excessive grooming. Most grooming in response to an itch creates a symmetrical pattern of baldness or damaged hair, with the cat accessing those areas it can comfortably reach on both sides. Any unilateral grooming that focuses on one site in particular may be in response to some trauma or unspecified pain in that specific area. Some skin cancers can result in irritation that is further complicated by excessive grooming and chewing of the affected site.

Diagnosis of the underlying medical cause of over-grooming is complex and may involve skin biopsies, food trials, blood tests and drug therapy. Veterinary surgeons in general practice usually pass these cases to a dermatologist, but any diagnosis and subsequent treatment is likely to benefit from a behavioural assessment to help manage your cat's stress at home.

Hunt the stress factor

If medical problems have been discounted, your cat's lifestyle should be assessed to ascertain what could potentially be seen as a source of stress. You should establish your cat's history of over-grooming to help identify any potential triggers at the time when it first started and look at how it progressed, how you or another owner responded and the general behaviour of your cat for clues to the underlying cause.

If the stressor can be identified and removed or modified, this may have a positive impact and reduce over-grooming in your cat. Your vet should also be consulted to judge whether anti-inflammatory drugs may be needed to break the itch–scratch cycle or antibiotics to treat any secondary bacterial infection.

If the trigger isn't obvious, it may still be useful to increase positive stimulation in the home by including regular play sessions, increasing challenging activities, food foraging and any opportunities for your cat to behave normally and instinctively 'cat-like'. If he is part of a multi-cat group, providing additional resources may put an end to any passive conflict that is going on undetected (see page 139). It's perfectly okay for you to distract your cat when he is grooming with positive activity such as play or anything that effectively prevents him from continuing.

THE PICA PROBLEM

Pica is the consumption of non-nutritious material, the most common manifestation being wool eating. The chosen material may vary, but the behaviour always involves repetitive chewing and mouthing with the back molar teeth.

Pica is seen most frequently in Siamese, Burmese and derivative breeds, and favoured delicacies include wool, rubber, plastic, leather and cardboard. Some cats stop short of actually swallowing and merely suck, chew or tear. If the cat takes the behaviour to the extreme, it will consume the material and risk emergency surgery to remove the resulting blockage from its intestines.

In many kittens this behaviour is present from a very early age, often arriving in their new home already chewing and sucking their bedding. Many grow out of the habit as they become adult, but for those with

Sucking on, chewing or tearing, and sometimes even swallowing, non-nutritious materials such as wool, rubber plastic and leather is called pica.

restricted lifestyles or susceptible to stress, it continues well into adulthood and is highly resistant to behaviour therapy. Researchers believe there is a genetic component to the problem and that, in some way, the susceptible cat's brain works slightly differently to others, suggesting that the act of chewing causes chemicals to be released in the brain, giving the recipient a feeling of intense pleasure. This then becomes addictive, and if you watch a cat 'wool eating', you will clearly see an expression of sheer ecstasy as it moves the material to its back teeth and chews.

Lock up your sweaters!

Cats that suffer from this compulsion are highly driven to seek out suitable materials to feed their habit and, if deprived in their own home, will search further afield and obtain the desired substance from other people's houses. If they are house cats they will raid laundry baskets, cupboards and drawers to find their favoured socks or sweaters.

This problem isn't the exclusive domain of the pedigrees, but they are certainly disproportionally represented in cases of pica. For example, Burmese often like to chew cardboard and even, alarmingly, electric cables. This presents a serious fire hazard and risk to life, and should never be considered a charming idiosyncrasy. Domestic non-pedigrees can also develop similar habits, indulging in rubber eating, plastic licking and cardboard tearing.

Not all pica habits represent serious addictions. If your cat is an idle chewer, try deterring him by using Olbas Oil (containing eucalyptus oil) or Bitter Apple (used to prevent animals from chewing at surgical sutures) to coat the item of choice, which is often effective. Removing the items from view that promote the behaviour may even be enough to manage the problem.

What else you can do

Many cats that develop this habit maintain it into adulthood if they have little or no access to outdoors. These cats need a great deal of stimulation indoors to give them things to do that are more rewarding than consuming leather or another unwise chewing choice. The ideal solution is free access outdoors, but if this isn't possible, a secured garden or outside pen is the second-best option (see pages 107–108).

Diets high in fibre that make your cat feel full may help to reduce his motivation to perform the behaviour, particularly if the items are invariably swallowed. Your vet will be able to recommend a diet that would be suitable for this purpose. Some cats benefit from the provision of cooked lamb or beef knucklebone with residual gristle and meat on them. However, cats that consume plastic and other man-made materials are not automatically drawn to something so obviously 'meaty'. Small dog hide chews can be attractive to some if they are soaked first in hot water and anointed with a few drops of fish sauce or a similar strong flavouring.

Although this behaviour is difficult to cure, it's still worth consulting a specialist, who will assess your cat's lifestyle and attempt to reduce or remove any significant stress-inducing factors. The referring veterinary surgeon may prescribe an antidepressant drug that will work alongside the behaviour therapy to 're-train' your cat's brain.

Pica can have a profound effect on your lifestyle as well as your cat's. It's very hard to live fabric free and almost impossible to deny your cat access to all the variety of potential targets. If you are considering the purchase of a Siamese, Burmese, Tonkinese or similar, it is advisable to enquire whether the problem has been evident in that particular family. As there is some evidence to suggest that pica can have an inheritable component, the responsibility lies with the breeders to be aware of it in their progeny and amend their breeding lines accordingly. If you have a cat that develops or maintains this habit, it's essential that you inform the breeder for just this reason.

MEDICAL WARNING SIGNS – PICA

Consumption or licking of non-nutritious material may indicate the presence of internal parasites or an inadequate or unsuitable diet.

Cats may consume other abnormal materials apart from wool and other fabrics in forms of behaviour that have no links with the habit that's commonly seen in Oriental breeds.

Unusual substances can be eaten or licked as a result of specific cravings associated with disease, such as hyperthyroidism, cancer, lead poisoning or feline infectious peritonitis (FIP). Cats struggling to cope with a severe burden of intestinal parasites or with chronic dietary deficiencies may also consume non-nutritious material.

WOOL–EATERS WARNING

The wool eaters discussed on pages 170–171 can also exhibit their own medical warning signs if the substance consumed doesn't pass through their gastrointestinal tract and instead forms a solid obstruction in the gut. Depending on the severity of the problem, it may be necessary to perform surgery and remove the obstruction directly from the intestines.

Sections of gut may also need to be removed in severe cases. Watch out for the following symptoms:

- *vomiting*
- *lethargy*
- *tense abdomen*
- *reduced or abnormal defecation*

Affected cats in these cases will not use the same shearing action associated with wool eating, nor will they exhibit the same look of euphoria that is seen in the Orientals, so it's fairly easy to distinguish one form of pica from another. Most cats eating for medical reasons will also exhibit other behaviour indicating that they are unwell.

Kittens can also be very exploratory with their mouths and often pick up objects and attempt to eat them. It's relatively common when kittens are first weaned and toilet trained, for instance, for them to eat litter. Some organic biodegradable materials will do no intrinsic harm, but many clumping clay litters are manufactured using a compound called sodium bentonite, a highly absorbent material that may cause dehydration and other complications if it's eaten or even inhaled by kittens. For this reason it's best to avoid the use of such litter materials when kittens are very young.

If your adult cat suddenly starts to eat clay-based litter, this can also indicate the presence of disease. Cats suffering from anaemia may lick or consume the litter, in which case veterinary intervention should be sought as a matter of urgency.

FAT CATS

Although obesity is not always considered as a 'behavioural problem', it can occur in cats, in the same way as with us, as a consequence of over-eating and under-exercising due to stress.

Obesity is one of the main health issues in adult cats leading to diabetes, liver and pancreatic disease, cardiovascular and joint disease and even

As with humans, cats become overweight as a consequence of overeating and under-exercising. Obesity is a key health issue in adult cats.

complications during surgery and anaesthesia. Many modern proprietary foods for cats contain large quantities of carbohydrate and this converts to glucose that is readily stored as fat if the calories taken in exceed the cat's nutritional requirements. Neutering cats, albeit a necessary procedure, will slow the metabolism and result in fewer calories being necessary to maintain body condition. Many cats have a sedentary lifestyle, living indoors or with limited access outside, and owners will often feed unmeasured quantities of highly palatable and calorie-dense food, supplemented by yet more food and titbits.

　　When your cat visits the vet every year for his annual check-up, he will be weighed and the vet will often assess his 'body condition score'. Weight in itself is not the best indicator, as some cats have smaller frames than others, so a visual assessment of your cat's body condition is more useful. Body

Neutering cats slows the metabolism, so fewer calories are needed to maintain body condition. Team this with a sedentary lifestyle and you have an overweight cat.

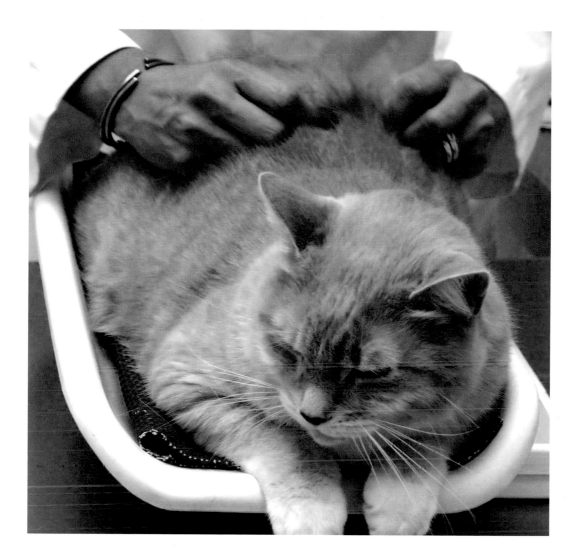

condition can range from emaciated to grossly obese; the ideal body shape is well-proportioned with an obvious waist behind the ribcage. The ribs should be felt under the skin, but not prominent enough to be seen. A flattened appearance over the back when observed from above would indicate that large pockets of fat are present either side of the spine. Cats with excessive body fat are not as flexible as they should be and many find it hard to reach all areas to groom efficiently. Obese cats often have dandruff in their coats and dirty bottoms. They are exercise intolerant and unable to jump up to any significant height but their condition can go unrecognized if owners just believe their cats are lazy. Studies show that some cats are at higher risk of obesity than others, the most susceptible group being non-pedigree neutered males who live indoors.

Light varieties are available in many foods that have all the nutrients your cat needs but fewer calories. Your vet may advise you to switch to one of these light diets or merely to reduce the amount of your cat's regular food or even start a formal weight-reduction programme.

If your vet considers your cat to be overweight, she may advise you to switch him to a light variety of food, one which contains all the necessary nutrients, but fewer calories.

THINKING SLIM

Any weight-reduction programme for your overweight cat will be supervised by your vet or a nurse in the veterinary practice who has been specially trained in obesity management.

First, your cat will be weighed accurately and his overall body condition assessed to establish the starting point. A target weight – this won't always be his ideal weight straight away if your cat is very obese – will be set and a date given to aim for, several months hence to ensure that the loss is gradual. If your cat loses weight too rapidly, muscle will be lost as well as fat. Your cat will then be weighed every week, on the same set of scales to ensure accuracy, to chart the progress. This enables the recommended calorie intake to be adjusted during the course of the programme. Sustainable, healthy weight loss is 1–2 per cent of the cat's total body weight per week as a maximum.

Balanced proprietary 'prescription' food is available for the management and reduction of obesity. Some contain high levels of fibre that increase the bulk of the diet and promote a feeling of fullness without adding calories. Others are based on higher levels of protein and a supplement that aids conversion of stored fat into a source of energy. A specific amount will be recommended as your cat's daily allowance and this should be divided into five or six portions and fed throughout the day. Use puzzle feeders to promote maximum activity and stimulation in your cat while he seeks out his food. Include play sessions at regular times to prompt frequent, short bursts of activity. Use fishing rod toys, small toy mice and catnip-infused prey-sized objects to encourage predatory behaviour. If access outdoors is available, encourage your cat to spend time outside. This can often be done by you simply choosing to spend more time in the garden.

Cats are capable of developing similar 'psychological hungers' to humans, indulging in eating as a safe, predictable and positive activity at times of stress. Failure to address these underlying psychological factors could result in no weight loss being achieved. Identifying stress triggers that could be contributing to a cycle of over-eating and inactivity may be challenging (see page 131), but tackling them is the key to successful weight management.

Never put your cat on a crash diet! Cats can develop hepatic lipidosis, a disease that is potentially life-threatening, if they are overweight and food is withdrawn rapidly.

BUBBLE'S FAT CLUB

Bubble had been on a weight reduction diet for six weeks but was not losing weight. A little detective work established that Bubble's had been snacking in neighbours' houses, polishing off any food that remained in the various cat bowls. A leaflet was sent to all the neighbours informing them of Bubble's 'fat club' enrolment and that his good health depended on him losing a significant amount of weight. Teri asked for all cat owners to remove any uneaten food from sight and to chase Bubble's out if he was caught pilfering. She also promised to keep everyone informed of his progress and for every gram of weight lost a donation would be made to the local cat rescue centre. This excited the locals and everyone was soon behind Bubble, encouraging him to stay on the straight and narrow and lose the necessary weight. Bubble is now a very healthy 4 kg (8½ lb) cat!

The dos and don'ts of cat care

Preventative care

Whether you are introducing a dog to your cat, going on holiday or expecting your first baby, it all needs careful thought, not just concerning the impact on the family but also your cat!

Offering solutions to problems that have arisen is helpful, but preventing them developing in the first place has got to be the way forward! So if you have a problem-free cat home or are considering the introduction of a feline to your family, this section is for you. There are certain decisions and actions involved that need to be considered carefully, as a wrong choice at this stage could herald the beginnings of a problem and a less than perfect life for your cat. With a little bit of forward planning you can reduce the risk of problems occurring and ensure your cat stays happy and healthy.

The right choice of cat, careful introductions and anticipating and avoiding potential triggers for stress (see pages 131–133) are all-important preventative measures. A cat's environment is of primary importance and the expression of its personality and potentially its stresses and strains will change dramatically depending on its context. Combine that with a social situation that is unsuitable, such as too many cats, and the cat's mood will plummet purely because of its circumstances. But place that same cat in a home as a singleton in an area where it's free to create a territory, and it will blossom and display all the elements of its personality that had previously been suppressed.

Unfortunately, there are times when you can inadvertently add to your cat's stress. Humans express their devotion in very specific ways: they focus on the object of their love, talk constantly and caress, hold and touch it frequently to reinforce the bond. Many cats with the appropriate upbringing will at best enjoy this attention and at the worst tolerate it with good grace. But not all cats are made the same and some will find the level of interaction distressing – see pages 90–96 for a quick lesson in how to communicate the feline way.

All these elements combine to create your cat's lifestyle, but there will still be specific circumstances that require a little practical guidance. Introducing a kitten or cat for the first time and anticipating occasions that could be stressful and taking the necessary precautions are the focus of this next section. Hopefully, this will enable you to be prepared for all situations!

COMMITTING TO A KITTEN

Preventing problems is all about planning ahead and the ideal place to start is before a new kitten is even acquired. Your family first need to sit down and discuss the implications of cat ownership.

It would take a robust kitten to cope with a lonely existence and little routine, as might be the case where family members are out at work and school all day.

Asking questions such as 'Does my lifestyle suit a pet?' and 'Can I afford to keep a cat?' seem obvious, but many of us embark on pet ownership with a great deal less consideration. If everyone is out at work or at school all day and your family's lifestyle is busy and chaotic, it would take a very robust and confident kitten to adjust to such a lonely existence with little routine. This would probably be a good situation to consider purchasing two siblings for company.

The cost is also a major consideration, not just food but healthcare, vaccinations, neutering, insurance, catteries and all the necessary equipment. If you have the option for a new cat to be allowed outside, your surrounding area should also influence the decision. If the area is already densely populated with cats, you may be inflicting a great deal of potential stress on any newcomer. The type of cat that's suitable for you and your household is also a consideration. Pedigrees may require greater maintenance, if they have a long coat for example, when daily grooming can become a chore to be avoided rather than a pleasure.

Once the decision is finally made, certain facts need to be established to ensure that your chosen kitten has had the necessary early experiences to prepare him for being a happy pet. Ideally, kittens should have been reared in a normal domestic setting with all the usual sights, sounds and smells that they are likely to experience when they leave to go to their new home. They should have been handled carefully after the age of two weeks by men, women and children to ensure that they understand the variety of shapes and sizes that humans come in. Regular veterinary examination and treatment for parasites such as intestinal worms and fleas is advised when rearing kittens, so you need to make sure, before you view the litter, that they have received all the necessary treatments.

Pedigree kittens tend to go to their new homes after an initial course of vaccinations at 13 weeks of age. Breeders of non-pedigree litters often want to re-home kittens as soon as possible, but leaving the mother before they are eight weeks old is not ideal for their optimum development and wellbeing in later life.

Choosing the right one

It's important that you have an opportunity to see the kittens with their mother, as nervous or shy mothers may influence their offspring to show equal timidity. Any kitten chosen should look healthy and display behaviour that indicates that he is confident in his response to his surroundings,

Ideally, kittens should have been handled by men, women and children and been reared in a normal domestic setting surrounded by the sights, smells and sounds that they will experience in your home.

other cats and people. The ideal kitten will have bright eyes with no sign of redness or discharge and clean ears free from dark brown wax that could indicate ear mites. His coat should be shiny and his belly should not be bloated, as this usually means that he has a significant burden of worms in his intestines. His anus should be free from any signs of diarrhoea and he should be active and playful.

THE HOMECOMING

You will need to prepare your home prior to the kitten's arrival to make it a safe environment for him, and from day one set routines that you intend to establish for the future.

Any gaps behind kitchen appliances and cupboards should be blocked and loose floorboards or gaps around pipes checked to avoid the kitten

When choosing your kitten, look for one with bright eyes with no sign of redness or discharge, clean ears free from brown wax, and a shiny coat.

squeezing through and being difficult to retrieve. Open fireplaces should be screened off, toilet lids closed and all external doors and windows closed securely to prevent escape.

All cleaning products, disinfectants, medicines and fragile ornaments should be placed in a secure cupboard. Potentially poisonous cut flowers or houseplants should also be removed just in case your kitten fancies experimenting with his diet and tries to eat them. Plants such as ivy, dumb cane (*Dieffenbachia*), poinsettia, cyclamen, hyacinth and lily are just some of the many that are potentially poisonous to cats and should be avoided. Any full-length curtains should be tied back temporarily to avoid the kitten from running up them and getting stuck at the top!

A single room should be equipped with food and water bowls, a litter tray of a suitable size for the kitten, scratching post and thermal bedding to keep the youngster warm. Any bed provided should have high sides to keep out draughts and a low front for easy access.

The whole family should also prepare for the kitten's arrival and understand that he will be very small and quick, and his tail and paws could easily be trodden on or trapped in closing doors if extra care isn't taken.

Bring the kitten to his new home with some of his old bedding if possible. It will be comfortingly familiar when all else is new.

Settling in

It's advisable to bring the kitten home with some bedding. This will act as a familiar, comforting object when everything else is new and can be placed in the kitten's new bed to encourage its use. Many owners feel that kittens needs to be close to them at night, particularly when they first arrive, but this can set an undesirable precedent for nocturnal games and excitement and no sleep for you! There is nothing cruel in putting a kitten 'to bed' in a cosy and secure environment until you wake in the morning, as long as the location and type of bed is right (see above).

The initial 24 hours should be a calm period of adjustment, so it's probably best for any children in the household to understand that the kitten should be left alone for a while. If the kitten seems receptive, then playing may relax him. However, if he disappears into a quiet hiding place, it's best to spend time in the room with him to accustom him to your presence and leave the cuddling for another day rather than coax him out.

Four to six small meals of a good-quality food specifically formulated for kittens should be offered each day at regular intervals. Any dietary change that you may wish to make after the kitten has arrived should be made gradually over a period of seven to ten days.

Kittens need their sleep when they are young, but will be very energetic in between with bursts of wild activity. Getting to know your kitten at this early stage is crucial to enable a bond to be created, so playtime and general interaction should take place during the times when he is naturally active and responsive.

KITTEN MEETS CAT

The introduction of a new kitten to the resident adult can either be trouble-free or fraught with danger! As there is such variation in their response, it's best not to take any chances.

Ensure that the household is quiet to reduce the risk of any additional stresses and avoid festive holidays or occasions when visitors are staying. Place a kitten pen – a wire cage of at least 1 m or 1 yd square – in the room in your home that your existing cat least favours. Allow the kitten to exercise within the room when the other cat isn't around. When the kitten is fed in the pen, the door to the room can be opened to allow your cat to investigate. Place a bowl of tempting food at a distance from the pen where your cat will eat comfortably. Make

MATCH MADE IN HELL

Domino, a lively Burmese kitten, was purchased as a companion for Dora, a sleepy and rather overweight middle-aged cat. When Domino arrived he made an immediate dash towards Dora, hissing and spitting, causing the older and previously clumsy cat to agilely scale the kitchen cupboards and land on top. The owners, believing that cats should be allowed to sort themselves out, left the two to get on with it. The following morning, when they found Dora still entrenched on the kitchen cupboard with Domino staring up at her, they decided the situation probably needed more time. A week later, with Dora still under siege and losing weight in an extremely rapid, unhealthy way, they wisely decided that this was not the perfect combination. Domino now resides happily with a relative and Dora is alone and exceedingly relieved. Not all matches are made in heaven.

this a daily routine, two or three times a day, and reduce the distance between the cat and the pen gradually until they are eating in a relaxed fashion either side of the pen wire.

A communal smell is always important within a cat group, so exchanging bedding between the two will allow them to become familiar with each other's scent and create a combination of their two odours. There is often a temptation to over-fuss your existing cat to compensate for the new arrival and indicate that your allegiance hasn't transferred to the kitten, but this can be stressful in itself if the amount of attention exceeds what your cat naturally enjoys.

After a week the kitten pen can be positioned in other rooms of increasing importance to your cat so that he understands that the kitten may be encountered in other areas of the home. Once the pen has travelled to a number of locations, and depending on the reaction from your cat, it may be possible to let them get to know each other after a couple of weeks. There may be the odd swipe, but it's always best to allow the cat and kitten to communicate unhindered unless the kitten is at risk of actually being

If you already have a cat, place the kitten in a pen in a room not much used by your existing cat. As cat and kitten become used to one another, move the pen to other rooms.

harmed. If this is the case, a cushion or pillow should be used to separate them rather than intervening with your hands to avoid injury.

KITTEN MEETS DOG

Your household's decision to acquire a kitten would ideally have been based on your pet dog's suitability, so it should be just a case of making the right sort of introduction.

Initially, the kitten should remain inside a kitten pen that is big enough for a bed, litter tray, food and water. Your dog should be allowed to explore the new kitten in the pen without the risk of injury or a chase ensuing if the kitten runs. The pen can then be moved from room to room for a couple of days at a time so that your dog can encounter the new arrival in different areas of the home.

The kitten and the dog should both be stroked daily to create a communal and familiar scent between them. In the early stages the kitten should be provided with exercise time outside the pen, with the dog shut out of the room for safety. The kitten should remain in the pen during interaction with the dog for several weeks, particularly if the dog is protective over his food, for example, and may respond aggressively towards the kitten at mealtimes. Once both kitten and dog seem relaxed together, the kitten can be held near the dog or allowed to approach with the dog on a lead to prevent any chasing. Treats can then be given to the dog if he remains calm.

Once the kitten is six months old, it should usually be safe to allow him to cohabit with your dog without supervision, providing all signs indicate that a friendship is developing. Make sure that the kitten has access to and from the house without having to come into direct contact with the dog's bed or feeding area. Provide high perches to give your kitten or any cat sanctuary and locate indoor litter facilities with care, as dogs are often keen to eat cat faeces and may hover in the vicinity and cause upset to your cat.

DID YOU KNOW...?

- *Flea treatment produced specifically for dogs can be lethal if used on cats. Toxicity can occur even if a cat comes into close physical contact with a dog that has recently been treated.*

- *Cats shouldn't be fed dog food as they have very specific nutritional requirements (such as an amino acid called taurine) and these are not met by the ingredients in your dog's diet.*

NEW DOG MEETS CAT

Any dog chosen should have a history of being brought up with cats or be a breed suitable for cohabiting with them. The sight hounds, such as Greyhounds, and many terriers are not ideal candidates.

The puppy or dog should be introduced to the home using a puppy pen or crate located in an area that doesn't block the cat from his chosen thoroughfares or access to food and essential resources. If you are introducing an adult dog, the pen can be used for quiet

Introduce a new
puppy to your cat in
a room from which
the cat can easily
escape. Avoid
unsupervised
encounters until
both animals seem
relaxed in each
other's presence.

times and sleeping. Ensure that there are plenty of high resting places where
your cat can retreat from the new arrival should he feel threatened at any
stage. It may also be useful to place a baby gate at the bottom of any stairs in
your home to give your cat the sanctuary of the upper floor.

The puppy should be introduced to your cat initially in a room from
which the cat can easily escape. If you hold the puppy and allow your cat
to approach, if willing, this will prevent any injuries should things get out
of hand. Let your cat then freely use the room where the puppy's pen is
located and they will soon get used to each other. When the puppy is out of
the pen it would be advisable to keep a long lead on his collar to stop him
from chasing the cat. Any unsupervised encounters should be avoided until
both parties are relaxed in each other's presence and the puppy has been
trained not to chase.

An adult dog should be fed a tasty treat in the pen before the cat is
brought into the room to investigate the newcomer. Give your cat attention
at this time by playing with him or offering his favourite food treat to
create a positive association with the new dog. When your cat appears to

relax in the dog's presence, you can open the pen and allow the dog to sit beside you, putting him on a lead to prevent him from chasing. If he remains calm, reward him with a food treat and praise. It is useful to train your dog to sit or stay on command to avoid the temptation of chasing the cat in the future.

NEW CAT MEETS OLD CAT

It will always be more difficult to introduce an adult to your existing cat. Confinement in a kitten pen can be distressing for an adult cat, so this introduction method is not advisable.

A single room can be used, but not a particular favourite of your existing cat, then introductions can be made gradually based on the three stages that would be followed if a cat naturally attempted to integrate into a new group.

During the first stage your cat will become aware of the odour of another cat. The new cat's scent can be collected and deposited in areas where your existing cat is housed and vice versa. Scent can be collected by stroking the cat around the cheeks, chin and forehead using a cotton glove or small cloth. This will collect small amounts of the naturally

Adult cats will find being confined to a kitten pen distressing, so keep a new cat in a separate room at first. When you bring old and new cats together, try not to interfere, unless there is the risk of injury,

secreted pheromones from the glands in the cat's face (see page 40 for the significance of this scent). This cloth can then be rubbed against doorways and furniture to enable both cats to explore the scent of the other without direct contact.

The second stage occurs when the two cats become aware of each other visually from a distance. This can easily take place if the door to the room is opened but both cats are prevented from crossing the threshold. A wood and wire frame can be constructed to fit within the door surround that will enable each cat to explore the other visually, if they want to, without the risk of physical harm. A baby's stair gate will give the same effect. Feeding either side of this barrier, at a distance that allows both cats to eat comfortably, will create positive associations between them. This is the perfect opportunity to move the new cat to a couple of other rooms, still using the wire frame, to ensure that the territory can be reasonably fairly divided once he is free to establish his own space.

The third and final stage can take place, depending on progress, after anything from one to several weeks with both cats having the opportunity to meet each other without barriers. Any interaction between them should be allowed to take place without interference from you unless they risk injuring each other.

Opposite Always supervise encounters with babies and toddlers. If you are expecting a baby, encourage friends with babies to visit to accustom your cat to the associated sights and sounds.

CAT MEETS BABY

The relationship with your cat will inevitably change when a new baby arrives. It can be a distressing time for him as routines change dramatically, new objects are introduced and you become less accessible.

Your cat's stress in this situation can, however, be reduced and even avoided altogether if you plan ahead. Several months before the baby is due, make the decision about where he or she is going to sleep at night. If the cot is initially going in your bedroom, then start denying access to your cat as soon as possible so that the transition doesn't take place abruptly the day baby comes home. Any designated nursery should be out of bounds at this stage so that it doesn't represent another change once the baby has been home for a few months. All the necessary accessories, such as buggies, cots and so on, should be introduced over a period of time to avoid a sudden increase in challenging smells and objects.

The baby's arrival will have a greater impact on your cat if he is kept exclusively indoors. Housebound cats are more sensitive to changes in their environment than those with free access outdoors. If your cat is used to having your undivided attention, it's important to gradually withdraw from him during the pregnancy, providing him with stimulation and more activity that will give him an interest outside his relationship with you. Consider all the new responsibilities that come with a baby and create a new cat routine that will fit in with those, including the necessary feeding, grooming and playing. If this routine is adopted as soon as possible, it will reduce the impact of the baby's arrival.

This is also a good time to encourage friends with babies to visit so that your cat becomes accustomed to the sights and sounds associated with them. Toddlers can be a little overwhelming for cats, so always supervise encounters and ensure that any handling is gentle. If your cat chooses to hide, allow him to do so rather than force him to interact.

KEEPING THE PEACE

The prevention of aggression breaking out between pet cats can potentially be achieved by avoiding overcrowded environments, both inside the home and within the wider territory outside as a whole.

The mix of characters chosen to form a multi-cat group need to be compatible, and once a stable group has been established, it's probably unwise to risk upsetting the balance by adding others (see pages 84–87).

The environment is also significant with some groups working well in one location and badly in another. It isn't possible, or even right, for your choice of home to be dictated by your cats, but it's probably worth looking at their requirements to limit the chances of problems occurring. Looking for parallels between feral colonies and multi-cat households, it's known that feral cats congregate together and form groups in areas where there is a plentiful and predictable food source and all other essential needs are available in sufficient numbers. If all these conditions are not present, the cats will disperse. Exactly the same applies to multi-cat households: the cats need to believe that there is enough for everyone and nothing is in scarce supply. As the members of the group reach social maturity they will interact or avoid each other, depending on their own preferences, and access to each resource will be divided with some degree of cooperation. Providing the personalities are fundamentally compatible, bearing in mind that some cats are instinctively more territorial and competitive than others, then aggression should be maintained at a normal and acceptable level.

Potential hot spots to avoid include multi-storey townhouses with narrow staircases to each level, which creates opportunities for single cats to easily block others from accessing important resources, small properties that cannot accommodate enough resources for the number

ONE CAT TOO MANY

Penny had successfully acquired six unrelated cats that all got on with each other. That is until number seven came along. The black cat, locally referred to as Lucky, had been a stray in the area for some time and had finally found his way into Penny's garden. She fed him and gradually tempted him to join the fold, after all, what problem was it to have one more? Sadly Penny had reached the point of "one cat too many". The previously harmonious group broke down in front of her eyes almost immediately, not only between the residents and the newcomer but amongst each other. Cats were fighting, pacing, spraying urine and soiling on beds and doormats, one even started to pull her fur out. Never before had Penny experienced such pandemonium. Fortunately she was wise enough to re-home Lucky and everything returned to normal, after a week or so.

of cats in them and homes with large expanses of glass that expose resident cats to the sight of a heavily populated external environment.

Unfortunately, you will always be a scarce resource, but don't attempt to divide your time and attention equally between each cat. This often creates more problems than it resolves, as the cats will have already decided where and when each has access and if *you* initiate contact outside that schedule, it may cause friction. If one of your cats is withdrawing from you at certain times then this may well be his choice under the circumstances.

Aggression between cats in a multi-cat household can often be minimized by trying to avoid overcrowding, both inside and out.

TROUBLE-FREE TRIPS

For your feline companion, journeys of any kind, particularly those that end up at the veterinary surgery, can be very stressful experiences if you don't take the right precautions.

If your cat wasn't exposed to car journeys as a young kitten, it's possible that they will continue to be a challenge for him throughout his adult life.

The cat carrier is often the first sign of trouble for your cat, so leaving it in a permanent and prominent location in the home, maybe with a soft bed inside, will prevent it from being a reason for your cat to escape every time it appears. A towel that has been previously used as a cat bed is useful,

Do not hide your cat carrier away when not in use; its reappearance can become a sign of trouble to your cat. Leave it around and accessible with comfortable bedding inside it.

as it can be used to cover the basket either during the journey or at the surgery while waiting in the reception area or at other times when there is much activity going on around him. This will provide a strong scent of home and familiar things, and may mask the other more challenging aromas of a typical busy vet practice.

It's always advisable for your cat to travel with a fairly empty stomach, as feeding just prior to a journey can result in 'accidents' and an unpleasant trip for everyone. The carrier should be lined with newspaper, polythene and a thick bed to ensure that any liquids produced will be appropriately absorbed. Secure the carrier in the car using the seat belt. Cats will often cry constantly during journeys, but comfort and reassurance may feel to them like a confirmation of their need to be anxious. A calm and normal demeanour during the journey will signal that you are not reinforcing the cat's fretful frame of mind.

If you are embarking on a long journey, the cat carrier should be big enough to accommodate a litter tray fixed to the base. Offer water regularly and keep the car well ventilated and at a comfortable temperature. Under no circumstances should you leave your cat in a car unattended for any length of time in warm weather.

NO-TEARS GROOMING

Some long-haired cats, such as Persians, need to be groomed daily to avoid matted clumps forming in their coats, which are extremely uncomfortable and often require removal by a vet under general anaesthetic or sedation.

Sadly, grooming a long-haired cat can be a distressing task, as not all cats love to be groomed, particularly in sensitive areas such as under the front legs and on the tummy. Breeders of long-haired pedigrees should always incorporate grooming into their programme of early socialization to ensure that the kittens become accustomed to this particular kind of handling and restraint from a young age. Unfortunately, it still remains a challenge for many owners.

If you have a cat that needs daily grooming but requires some persuasion, there are steps you can take to increase your cat's tolerance and acceptance of this essential maintenance. Your cat can be trained to accept grooming sessions of gradually increasing duration if the act is positively reinforced each time it occurs. You need to find a small food titbit or treat that your cat absolutely loves – but check with your vet first that it's an

'approved snack'! Once you have established the favourite morsel, this will be the reward for grooming and will only ever be offered during brushing and combing.

Choose a quiet room and a table top to make the process easy. Positioning it near a window may provide your cat with some interesting visual distraction. Start gradually, using gentle strokes of a comb through the fur from head to mid-back, for about ten seconds. Immediately afterwards, offer a treat and some praise and allow your cat to leave. Build up the time daily in five-second increments and each day move the comb over other parts of the body, starting with the face, sides and tail, then progressing to the base of the tail (over the hips) and eventually those difficult areas under the neck, behind each leg and on the tummy. Each session should finish with praise and the special food treat.

STRESS-FREE CELEBRATIONS

There are various times during the year when family and friends get together for celebration and merriment, but changes to normal routines and the introduction of new things and different people all represent potential challenges to your cat. Cats that are kept exclusively indoors are particularly sensitive to changes of this kind, so they will need to be considered when festivities are planned. Those with free access outdoors may seize the opportunity to escape, but care should be taken to ensure that they don't feel unable to return to the home due to the presence of others. Your cat may need somewhere safe and quiet to escape the noise and excitement. Guest

Breeders should try to incorporate grooming into early socialization to ensure that kittens become accustomed to it. Carry out grooming on a table top near a window to give your cat something to watch.

Opposite Start with very short sessions and build up the time daily. Always finish with praise and a food treat that is offered only after grooming.

bedrooms are often a chosen refuge for shy cats, but the arrival of visitors means that favoured areas may not be available at the very time they are needed. Careful selection of alternative havens away from thoroughfares or the hub of the activity should be made and the locations provided with a warm bed to represent a sanctuary where your cat can remain undisturbed.

Any celebration may come with fireworks, so if your cat has access outdoors, keeping him in when it gets dark during the appropriate season will ensure that he remains safe. Curtains should be drawn as it gets dark and playing music or having a television or radio on can mask the sounds of any fireworks. If you have prior knowledge of a local firework event taking place, it's probably advisable for you to remain indoors that night, just in case. However, you are not there to reassure your cat; it's much more useful to remain calm and act normally. Your cat's favoured hiding places should be accessible and any temptation to check on him if he retreats there should be avoided. Provide an indoor litter tray in a convenient location, although anxious cats often avoid toilet visits if they feel threatened.

If your cat becomes extremely agitated in response to the loud bangs of fireworks, speak to your veterinary surgeon in advance of the season so that any medication or supplement that may be helpful can be prescribed ahead of the event.

VACATIONS AND MOVES

Family vacations represent a dramatic disruption to normal routines for a cat, and moving house is potentially traumatic for a territorial creature, so making these processes as stress-free as possible will help your cat adjust.

The best option for your cat regarding his care when you are away will depend on his personality. If he's a confident cat who spends a significant period of time outside in his territory, it may be appropriate to allow him to remain there. This suits some individuals very well and a kind neighbour or friend can visit twice a day to feed and tend to his needs until you return. Other cats that are not quite so emotionally independent will see your departure as a huge burden of responsibility on them to defend the home alone. Strangers visiting at random times will merely compound their anxieties. These cats are probably better catered for at a reputable, compassionate and secure cattery.

Recommendations of good establishments locally are worth pursuing, but always check for yourself when making a decision about your cat's care. Popular catteries will always get booked up early, so be prepared to do the groundwork far in advance of your away time.

Opposite When there are changes to the household routine such as overnight guests or celebrations, try to keep your cat's favoured retreats accessible and resist disturbing him if he is there.

If you need to board your pet in a cattery, always look around it first, taking particular note of the condition of cats there at the time. Whenever possible, go by personal recommendations.

Opposite When moving, designate one room at either end to keep your cat, and his possessions, in while the move takes place. It may be easier to board him in a cattery for a night or two.

Try to choose establishments that only board cats. Make an appointment to view a cattery, and if the owner refuses to show you the premises, look elsewhere! The surroundings to the premises should be neat and clean and the cat accommodation for each pen should have a separate enclosed and insulated sleeping area and an individual exercise run. The enclosed area should be secure, and dry and warm in the winter and cool in the summer. The entire pen should be big enough to accommodate food, water, scratching posts, litter tray, toys and exercise. The pens should have 'sneeze barriers' between each unit and all areas should be free from odours and be well maintained. There should always be two locked doors between your cat and freedom to ensure that no 'guests' are accidentally allowed to escape.

The cats in residence when you visit should look alert and interested, with empty food bowls to suggest that their appetites are good and they have adjusted well to the strange environment. If you are satisfied that it's a good cattery, it may be worth trying a long weekend to start with, to ensure that your cat is as happy with the establishment as you are.

Move management

When moving house, your cat should be protected as much as possible from the frantic activity on the actual day of the move, so it's best to shut him into one room that has been cleared of all large furniture, where you can leave food, water, bedding, litter tray and other familiar items. The removal team will need to know that the door to this room must remain shut to avoid him going missing at the last moment. You can also ask them to unload the furniture for one room first at the new home so that your cat can be placed somewhere safe the other end.

Once the removal team have packed up everything and left, your cat can be taken to your new home and placed in the designated room with all his familiar objects to explore at his own pace. Exploring further will be possible once all the furniture is in place and everything is peaceful. He may show some trepidation at this point, but if the furniture is familiar it will give him some confidence to investigate his new environment. All windows and the door should remain firmly closed just in case he becomes disorientated and attempts to escape. However he responds to his new home, be relaxed and don't reinforce any anxious behaviour with reassurance.

It may be difficult to confine your cat for the recommended period of two to three weeks, so if he is normally allowed outside and is keen to get out, choose a weekend when you are at home and open the door for the first time just before a mealtime so that you can be confident that he will be hungry fairly soon.

If you just can't bear having to worry about your cat as well as everything else on the day of the move, arrange beforehand for him to have a day at a local cattery, away from all the hustle and bustle.

Index

Acknowledgements

Author acknowledgements

I would like to thank my agent, Mary Pachnos, for her continued support and good humour and the team at Hamlyn for their enthusiasm and guidance. I have juggled many balls while writing this book and Clare Hemington (my amazing practice manager), all my lovely clients and colleagues, friends and family have all shown great tolerance when I have been, from time to time, rather distracted. Thank you most of all to Charles and Mangus, who bear the brunt of my preoccupation with all things feline!

Publisher acknowledgements

Executive Editor: Trevor Davies
Senior Editor: Lisa John
Deputy Creative Director: Karen Sawyer
Designer: Mark Stevens
Picture Researcher: Zoë Spilberg
Senior Production Controller: Amanda Mackie

Picture acknowledgements

Alamy/Peter Alvey 67; /Robert Ashton/Massive Pixels 22; /David Askham 185; /Lena Ason 166; /avatra images 12; /Sigitas Baltramaitis 128; /blickwinkel/Moch 141; /blickwinkel/Schmidt-Roeger 78; /Bubbles Photolibrary 63; /Adam Burton 82; /De Klerk 130; /Mark Duffy 187; /Wendy Farrow 14; /Isobel Flynn 146; /Alex Griffiths 103; /imagebroker/Jürgen Lindenburger 48; /imagebroker/Konrad Wothe 134; /Neal and Molly Jansen 192; /Johner Images/Stefan Wettainen 4, 109; /Juniors Bildarchiv 75, 132, 155, 191, 195; /Emma Lee/Life File Photo Library Ltd 26; /Stephen Parker 201; /ReimarRalph 198; /Frances M. Roberts 98; /Mark Scheuern 102, 117; /Doug Schneider 30; /Steppenwolf 81; /Dan Sullivan 200; /Jack Sullivan 126; /Tierfotoagentur/D. M. Sheldon 154; /vario images GmbH & Co.KG/McPhoto 32; /Rob Walls 21. **Ardea**/John Daniels 110, 121, 149, 152, 203; /Jean Michel Labat 159, 162, 173. **Corbis** 85, 125; /Janie Airey/cultura 91; /DLILLC 53; /Fotofeeling/Westend61 11; /Julie Habel 39; /Frank Lukasseck 54; /Peter Mintz/Design Pics 74; /Alan Marsh/Design Pics 138; /Robert Pickett 70; /Benjamin Rondel/First Light 161. **Dorling Kindersley**/Marc Henrie 25. **Fotolia**/Henrik Winther Andersen 174; /Marilyn Barbone 177; /Mark Bond 1; /Brenda Carson 101; /crzy77 47; /Sebastian Duda 172; /Dominik Eckelt 181; /galbertone 95; /Hiro 113; /Jelu 52; /Irina Karlova 164; /Scott Latham 27; /Kathy Libby 51; /Catherine Murray 35; /Niza 16; /Carlos Nobre 156; /oldu 105; /Piccolo 90; /Kirsty Richards 151; /SBL 184; /Robert Scoverski 129; /skubird 112; /Simone van den Berg 116; /Oscar Williams 175; /Igor Zhuk 122, 122, 145; /Dušan Zidar 13. **Getty Images**/altrendo images 41; /Jane Burton 69, 118; /Wayne Eastep 73; /GK Hart/Vikki Hart 64; /Image Source 97; /MIXA 182; /Natasha Japp Photography 189; /PHOTO 24 71; /Justin Sullivan 169. **Masterfile**/Bill Frymire 8, 15; /David P. Hall 19; /Minden Pictures 49. **Nature Picture Library**/Jane Burton 59; /Jose B. Ruiz 37; /Ulrike Schanz 165. **Photolibrary Group**/age fotostock/Harald Braun 2, 106; /age fotostock/Morales Morales 33, 183; /BSIP Medical/May May 60; /BSIP Medical/OLIEL OLIEL 199; /Juniors Bildarchiv 29, 40, 43, 93, 94, 114, 115, 137, 143, 170, 190, 196; /LOOK-foto/Konrad Wothe 133; /Mauritius/Layer Layer 86; /Nordic Photos/Lasse Pettersson 142; /Oxford Scientific (OSF)/Alain Christof 38; /Oxford Scientific (OSF)/Nick Ridley 178; /Oxford Scientific (OSF)/Satyendra Tiwari 44; /Pixtal Images 120; /Robert Harding Travel/Walter Rawlings 57; /Tips Italia/Bildagentur RM 18; /Vstock 153. **Photoshot**/Imagebroker.net 77; /Imagebrokers 7, 88; /NHPA/Jane Knight 157.